Flanders Bottom
Latimers
Well Wood
Cheyneſs
Hill Farm
Loudham Farm
Loudham Lane
Cheyneſs Lodge
Burtons
New Houſe
Charley Wood
Lane
Rough Wood Farm
Shire
Vach
Newland
Horn Hill
St. Giles
Pawlings
End
Shiplings
Tatlers
Shire
PART OF HARTF
42
41
40
39

A HISTORY OF
LITTLE CHALFONT

A HISTORY OF LITTLE CHALFONT

BY

IVOR WHITE

Ivor White

LITTLE CHALFONT RURAL PRESERVATION SOCIETY

Published by The Little Chalfont Rural Preservation Society,
Buckinghamshire, England.

Printed and Designed by:
Alpine Press Ltd, Kings Langley, Hertfordshire

Jacket design by Marjorie Simpson and Alpine Press Ltd

Text set in ITC Century Book 11 on 13 point

Front end papers: *John Rocque's Map of Berkshire, Oxfordshire and Buckinghamshire 1763.*

Rear end papers: *Sketch map showing plots of land offered for sale in 1920.*

Front cover: *"Corner of the Village Green" by Marjorie Simpson.*

Re-printed 1996

ISBN 0 9521886 0 0

Contents

Acknowledgments....3

Introduction....5

Old Buildings....13

The Turnpike Road....27

The Tithe Map....43

The Metropolitan Railway Line....49

The Start of The Village....59

Local Firms and Telephones....75

War Time....87

The Old and New Village Halls....97

Developments since the End of War....101

Schools and Churches....111

Miscellany....119

Little Chalfont Rural Preservation Society....127

Sources....128

Sponsors....129

Dates....133

Index....136

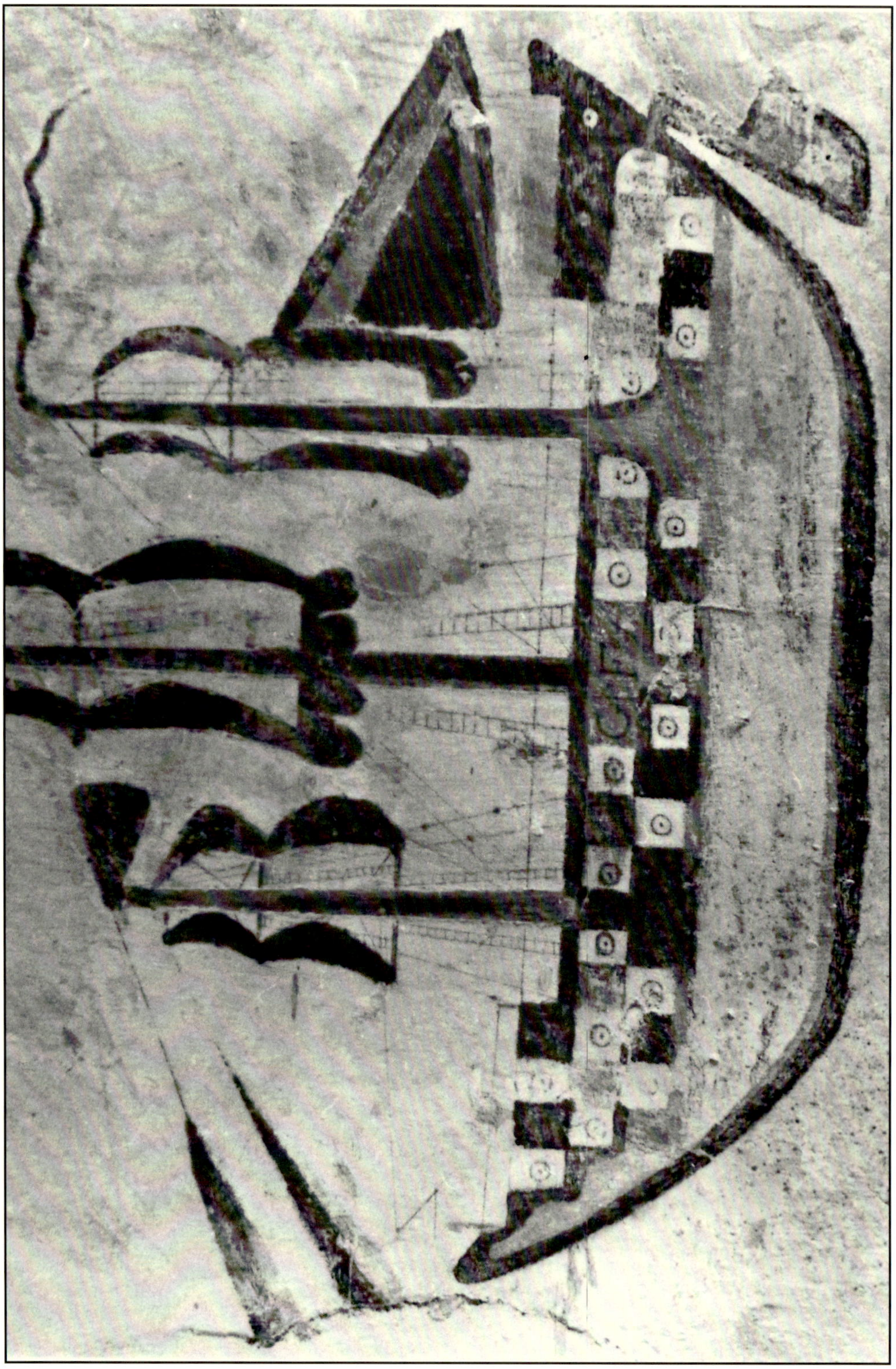

Wall painting hidden behind plaster in one of the rooms at Beel House Nurseries.
Said to date from about 1730, the artist's name, G. Foy, is seen below the central mast.

Acknowledgments

I would like to offer my grateful thanks to all who have contributed information and material for this book. I would especially like to thank Frances Ashdown who generously allowed me to use her own local history research notes and material, and Marjorie Simpson who drew the beautiful illustrations, including the picture on the front cover. Colin Seabright has an extensive collection of old postcards, and he kindly permitted me to use those which are of local interest.

Father Gerard Collins, who has made a detailed study of Beel House and its occupiers, supplied most of the information about the house. Nancy Thomas, a historian who has lived in the village most of her life, suggested various sources for further research and provided the story about the wartime bombers. Anne Hearne and Doris Chaney, explained what it was like being telephone operators in the village post office. Evelyn Lovell kindly supplied material about Grimsdell's Tomb, and allowed me to decipher the old inscription.

Peter Marston and Ray Edmunds helped with the story of Statters; Christian and Judy Hojsgaard, and George and Mona Hance supplied the information about The Piece and Beel House Nurseries; and Christopher North offered a considerable quantity of legal documents concerning the sale of extensive tracts of land along the main road and in Burtons Lane; Doreen Wright provided the fascinating aerial photograph taken by her husband in the 1930s, and Phyllis Harriss related stories about her father, the Finch Lane chimney sweep.

Anecdotes, many of them pre-war, were told by Ivy Wheeler, Joan Adamson, Kathleen Montey, David Lofts, Gladys Swain; Gary May let me have his paper on the history of Harewood Downs, and Peter Wilcockson contributed information from his research on Beel House. Peggy Palmer and Mary Everett of the Chess Valley Archaeological and Historical Society gave much good advice.

I am also indebted to the staff at the British Library, the County Records Offices at Aylesbury, Bedford and Reading, the Buckinghamshire Museum, the London Transport Museum, the Greater London Records Office, Rickmansworth Library and our own libraries at Chesham, Amersham and Little Chalfont, all of whom were unfailingly helpful and patient. Permission to use maps, photographs and articles was given by the Bucks Examiner, the Record Offices at Aylesbury and Reading, the County Museum, London Transport Museum, Buckinghamshire Archaeological Society and the Ordnance Survey. Ronald Mitchell allowed me to use an aerial photograph taken only recently.

Finally, my special thanks to my wife Deirdre and my daughter Frances for checking numerous drafts and suggesting a number of improvements to the text; and to my son Duncan, for making the initial layout of the book using the LaTex text processing system. To all of these, and many others, my grateful thanks for all their help.

Hatfield to Reading mile post near Church Grove; made by John Wilder of Reading in 1822 for the Turnpike.

Introduction

Many people living or working in Little Chalfont have admired the beautiful display of daffodils which line the grass verges from one end of the village to the other in springtime, and have also appreciated the recent improvements around the village green. Flowering trees have been planted quite extensively, a heather and conifer border has been created, snowdrops and crocuses have been massed together and various seats have been placed around the green. These changes were due to the efforts of the Rural Preservation Society, and were funded from member's subscriptions with valuable assistance from a major local firm. Most of the work has been carried out during the last five years.

When this programme of plantings was nearing completion, the Society cast around for ideas for its next project, and eventually decided to attempt to write something about the history of the village. This book is the outcome.

When asked about the origins of Little Chalfont, most people would reply that it is just a modern settlement which has grown up around the railway station; this, of course, is substantially true. But in searching into the past, information has been uncovered about, for example, the old Turnpike Road and a possible Toll House, the stopping up of certain ancient roads and the opening of others, and the existence of an old tomb.

From the start, the question arises as to what should rightly be called Little Chalfont, and which parts of the district should be included in any history. Strictly speaking, the name applies simply to one of the wards of the Parish of Amersham, administered by the Amersham Town Council. Other parts, however, lie within the Parish of Chalfont St. Giles, and many would say these should also be included. A further complication is that until the 1930s, the land around the station, including Village Way, was part of the Parish of Chenies. No help can be obtained from the past, since less than a hundred years ago, no settlement existed which could conceivably be called a village, and there is no compelling reason why the name of Chalfont should be associated with the district.

The author, therefore, has chosen to cover an area rather wider than simply the ward of Little Chalfont, in justification of which it need only be cited that very few local residents know where the exact boundary between Little Chalfont and St. Giles lies. Some would suggest that the village consists of the island of built-up land surrounded on all sides by the green belt, which can be clearly seen on an aerial photograph.

To the north of the village runs a ridge of land overlooking the Chess valley, which has been clothed with beautiful beech woods for many centuries. In a report[1] written at the beginning of the nineteenth century, the surveyor states: 'As the woods are not only ornamental, but profitable in their present disposition, the continuation of the plan of planting them up after every fall, is a most salutary measure, and should never be neglected.' It is comforting to know that this advice is still being acted upon in present times, as witness the replanting programme carried out by the Forestry Commission about thirty years ago.

In the early eighteenth century, the road from Amersham to Chenies and Rickmansworth was narrow, twisting, rutted and overhung with trees, and it was not until the second half of the century that improvements were slowly brought about. Amersham Common covered an extensive tract of land stretching from Bell Lane through Chesham Bois towards Hyde Heath, criss-crossed by numerous tracks and paths. A small settlement consisting mostly of cottages began to be established along the side of the common, taking the name of Amersham Common - often shortened to The Common - and a few cottages were also built by Finch Lane marking the end of the open land.

Apart from these isolated groups, virtually all other buildings consisted of farmhouses such as Colemans, Snells, Cokes, Loudhams, Wilmotts and Hill Farm (later called Old House Farm), some of which had clusters of adjacent dwellings for the workers. These farmhouses, together with the surrounding land, were owned by important landowners such as the Duke of Bedford and the Cavendish family, and were leased to tenant farmers, some of whom retained the tenancy through several generations. But by far the most im-portant property was Beel Park, lying just beyond the Common; the date of the present house is uncertain, the deeds having been lost two hundred years ago, but it has been said that there was an earlier building dating from medieval times.

Development of the village was commenced in the early 1920s, resulting in a somewhat haphazard pattern, described in a County Council survey[2] of 1964 as: 'The sprawl of development, wasteful and untidy, leaving gaps committed for future building'. The survey led to the production of a Little Chalfont Town Map, together with a statement of overall policy, and the modern layout follows these recommendations closely. It is interesting to note, from this report, the growth of population from the turn of the century:

Year	1901	1911	1921	1931	1951	1958	1974
Population	150	200	350	800	2250	5125	6215

Today, with the population rising towards 7000, most residents hope that, with the discipline imposed by the green belt, the numbers may stabilise at that level. Many are already unhappy about the urbanisation of the village which has taken place within the last two decades, as this poem written by Elizabeth Jane Stewart expresses:

Let's develop Little Chalfont
They said with mighty glee.
Let's make it big like Neasden
Great Chalfont it will be.

They set to work
They made some plans
The residents were cross
But then it wasn't up to them
The architect was boss.

So they built up Little Chalfont
Some were sad to see it go.
But then the architect had said
The little town must grow.

It grew quite large and ugly too
With buildings everywhere
And factories with lots of smoke
To pollute the country air.

The architect was very pleased,
He said, 'That will suffice,
Although I say it all myself
It does look rather nice.'

'I've built up Little Chalfont
Now a lovely town you see,
I'm sure the residents are pleased
And all because of me.'

It is hoped that this book will convey some of the flavour of the district before the coming of the railway, and of the subsequent development, slow at first, but reaching a climax after the war. There will inevitably be gaps in the story, since documentation of bygone times is patchy, and the author would very much like to hear from anyone who can fill in any missing parts.

Loudham's cottages on the corner of Burtons Lane which were demolished in 1967.

The White Lion Road and Inn, taken about the turn of the century.

The White Lion Inn. Decorated for the Coronation of King Edward VII in 1901. Advertising lunches, teas and accommodation for ladies. William George Harris, second on the right, was killed in a steam engine accident in Bell Lane.

A view in Finch Lane about 1920.

The Pineapple Inn about 1910.

A cycle outing along the White Lion Road, postmarked February 5th, 1911.

The Pineapple Inn sign can just be seen beyond the two little girls.

The old Amersham Common Post Office with the Pineapple Inn sign beyond, taken about 1910.

Scouts on parade in the White Lion Road near Bell Lane before the First World War, with the officer riding a cycle. The railway line can just be discerned on the right.

The White Lion Road at Amersham Common taken after road widening in about 1925. The petrol garage has since been modernised.

Old Buildings

The few old buildings still extant consist of farmhouses, workers' cottages, the estate house of Beel Park, and a possible Toll House; there is also a tombstone of the Grimsdell family. All the farms were owned by large landowners who leased them to tenants, some of whom worked the land from father to son. Very little information about the farms seems to have survived, although the names of some of them appear on seventeenth-century documents. Thus this chapter will describe only those for which records have been discovered. Further research may bring more to light.

GRIMSDELL'S TOMB

Lying in the garden of a house in Cokes Farm Lane is a tombstone bearing the following inscription:

> Within this place lies the bodies
> of Mr. Richard Grimsdell who purchased
> this estate and died in 1657 and
> his wife. Of Mr. Richard Grimsdell his
> son who died in 1716 aged 64. And Jane
> his wife who died in 1730 aged 86.
> Of Mr. Richard Grimsdell the onley son of
> Mr. Richard Grimsdell by Jane his wife
> who died in 1712. And left issue
> 4 daughters coheirs of this estate.
> And of Mrs. Jane Grimsdell one of the coheirs of the
> said Mr. Richard Grimsdell by Hannah his wife aged
> 32. In memory of whom his affectionate wife hath
> erected this stone in 1739.

In a letter to his uncle,[3] William Lowndes writes in December 1859:

> It appears that there were entries made at the time in the Parish Register, as the following extracts will show, though the name is spelt differently in two of them:
>
> 1716.....Richard Grimsdale, buried in woolens.
> 1730.....Jane Grimsdell, buried in her orchard.
> 1739.....Jane Grimsdale, spinster, buried in an orchard.
>
> The tombstone was formerly surrounded by a wall four and a half feet high, all traces of which have now disappeared. About fifty years ago some trees, which are still standing, were planted round the burial ground, close to the foundation of the wall.

Within two days of the above letter being written, another one on the same topic was sent from Latimer Rectory by Bryant Burgess to Mr. Lowndes, saying:

> I went yesterday to look at the tombstone of the Grimsdells. I know of no reason for these strange burials: but the date of the first interment at Cokes Farm (1647) suggests to my mind what may be a clue to the whole question. In those troublous times, in which we know that party spirit ran very high in the country, it would seem not unlikely that Grimsdell, with perhaps a prejudice against the service, and a dislike to consecrated ground as connected with the idea of prelacy, might choose to be buried in that picturesque spot on his own property. The spot close by the house, and overlooking a beautiful valley among the hills, is just such an one as a man might stand on day by day, until with the peculiar notions we have imagined, he might fancy it for his body's resting place. The head of the family being buried there, and a vault made, the descendants, brought up with the same opinions, might choose to be buried there also; and then Mr. Liberty of Chorley Wood (whose name may have had its origin in the free-thinking propensities of the family) may have admired the spot and the peculiarity of such a place of burial; and so have resolved upon a similar tomb for himself in his own field two miles away.
>
> Now this is all my supposition only, but it appears to me the most likely solution of the mystery. In the case of the Grimsdells, the proximity of 'Chapel Field' seems to point the other way; but there is no sign that I can find of any other interment there, and the wording of the inscription is different from what we would expect to find in a Churchyard.

The actual date on the tombstone has recently been found to be 1657 not 1647. The Liberty Tomb mentioned lies on the side of the public footpath from Latimer to Chenies about a quarter of a mile from the river bridge at Latimer. It has been suggested that the Grimsdells were Quakers and did not wish to be buried on church ground.

Grimsdell's tomb.

The Lodge near Grimsdell's tomb in Cokes Farm Lane in about 1910.

BEEL HOUSE

Beel House, which is situated between Finch Lane and Dr. Challoner's High School for Girls, was occupied in 1954 by the famous actor Dirk Bogarde. He has described part of his time there in his book 'Snakes and Ladders'. His friend Tony Forwood lived at Bendrose Farm, and when Bogarde heard that the Forwoods wished to acquire more land, he offered to take part of the Beel Estate. For the sum of £4000, the house together with seven acres was purchased. With the help of a local builder, the east wing of eleven rooms was demolished, and blocked windows were opened up. There was at that time a conservatory, which ran along the south terrace, filled with palms, geraniums and other exotic plants; it also housed an aviary of tropical birds. The actress Kay Kendall used to call it the 'outpatients department'. It is said that Alan Lerner first met Rex Harrison at Beel House to discuss the future production of 'My Fair Lady'. When the girls' school was built, it was natural that the famous man should become the centre of attraction. So to prevent the girls gathering by the fence of the house, a large bank of soil was built and planted with shrubs. But after eight years the house was sold and he moved from the district.

The age of Beel House is uncertain, but the following extract from an article by G R Elvey in the Records of Buckinghamshire (Vol. 16) throws some light on its origins:

> A larger tract of land ... stretches to the Chalfont (St. Giles) boundary. On it we notice the names of Reeves Farm, Little Reeves and Beel House. Beel I take to be a corruption of Bedel, and men of that name lived in the parish in the 13th century, and for two hundred years thereafter. If land and buildings had to be found for the lord's reeves and for his beadle, the most likely place would be on the lord's desmesne, and this land was probably part of his desmesne manor.

The estate is said to have been owned, during Henry VIII's reign, by one of the Dukes of Buckingham - a descendant of the Mandeville family which had acquired Amersham after the Conquest. Father Gerard Collins, who was the priest at St. Aidan's Catholic Church for many years, has undertaken a detailed study into the history of the house,[4] and a copy of his research is deposited at the County Records Office in Aylesbury. He states that the original Deeds were missing, and could not be found, when the property was sold to William Lowndes of The Bury, Chesham, in 1836.

Mary Pennington, the wife of Isaac, was one of the early Quakers. She was the mother, through an earlier marriage, of Gulielma Springett who was courted by and married to William Penn who later, as Governor, founded the

State of Pennsylvania in America. All histories about the early Quaker days say that the Penningtons came to live in Woodside House in Amersham (on the site of the present-day swimming pool), and that after Mary's death in 1682 it passed to her son John. Father Collins, however, has developed a fascinating thesis, that Woodside was not in Amersham, but a house of the same name which later became known as Beel House. By studying legal documents associated with nearby farms such as Reeves, Bendrose and Wilmotts, as well as the Lowndes Estate, he has concluded that Beel House was indeed the Penningtons' home. For example, John Pennington in his will, dated 31st May 1708, bequeathed:

> ... all that messuage or tenement wherein I now dwell called Beale House with all the lands and appurtenances to my brother Daniel Wharley and Thomas Elwood of Coleshill in the parish of Amersham.

No documents have been found to suggest that John Pennington sold any house in Amersham, or purchased Beale House, and the conclusion seems to be that Woodside House was the one now known as Beel House.

Map of Amersham Common 1816.

In 1769 Kender Mason, who later became a substantial landowner in the district, bought Beel House; in 1787 he added to his estate by acquiring Cokes, Reeves and Abbotts Farms. Kender Mason never occupied the house himself, but his sons and grandsons lived there until it was sold to William Lowndes in 1836. Mason's two sons, Henry William (who later adopted his mother's name of Pomeroy), and Kender, a Lord Lieutenant of the County, were among those who benefited from the enclosure of Amersham Common in 1816.[5]

At this time, they proposed that Finch Lane running down to the lower road into Amersham should be stopped up; and also that the Amersham to Uxbridge Road, which led from the Common via part of Finch Lane and through Beel Park next to the House, should be closed. They were successful in the latter plan, but Finch Lane remained open to traffic.

The name of Lord Nelson is linked to Beel House. The grandson of the original Kender, Lt. Henry William Mason, High Sheriff of Buckinghamshire, took as his second wife Horatia Matcham, the daughter of Lord Nelson's second sister Catherine. There were three children of this marriage: George Nelson, Susan Augusta and Horatio Nelson, the latter dying at only nine months.

After the acquisition of the house in 1836 by William Lowndes, it was let to a succession of tenants, but in 1861 was recorded as being dilapidated. Father Collins has compiled a tentative list of the occupants, which includes Mr. A. A. Lyle of the Tate and Lyle sugar family who lived there for four years from 1911. He was responsible for putting in the extensive oak panelling, and also electricity in the coach house, said to be the first in the village. Before then, Dennis and Frances Milner occupied the house from 1871, and an extract from a newspaper report in 1892 gives a flavour of Victorian times:[6]

> Children from the National School at Amersham Common had their annual treat in Beel House Park on Saturday. Although the schools have been closed owing to a prevalence of measles, nearly every child was able to be present. About 3.30 tea was provided, and everyone did ample justice to the plentiful supply of tea, bread and butter and cake. A dispersion was then made to the swings, cricket etc, which were indulged in until between 6 and 7. At that time, Mrs. Milner gave every child a present, the gifts consisting of useful articles of clothing, including flannel, print, calico, shirting, stockings etc. Scrambling for gooseberries, gingerbreads and sweets then followed; then more games, and after a second sitting down to more bread and butter, tea and cake, and three hearty cheers for Mrs. Milner for her kindness, a start was made for

Beel House in the early part of the century.

Beel House, 1993.

home, all having thoroughly enjoyed themselves. This is only another of the many instances of Mrs. Milner's generosity and interest which she has displayed on behalf of the Amersham Common Schools. Before closing, a word should be said in praise of the lawns and gardens, which are now in the highest state of beauty and perfection, reflecting great credit on Mr. Charles Olney, the head gardener.

In the early 1950s, it was reported in the local paper that:

> The residents of White Lion Road and Finch Lane were strongly represented when they joined force with the Amersham RDC and Bucks County Council in opposing an application by Mr. W. G. Lowndes to turn Beel House Park Estate into a private development estate. Twenty five residents were represented, and the application was turned down. At the hearing the chief engineer of the local waterworks was heard to remark that "the water is not adequate at the White Lion Public House". What could he have meant?

Much more recently, Mr. Bryn Williams carried out substantial renovations and additions, which included a new block at the rear. He also introduced a herd of deer into the park, and in less than ten years they have increased in number from the original ten to over forty. The latest owner is the pop singer 'Ozzy' Osbourne, who spends most of his time in America giving concerts and making recordings.

THE SHEEP COTTAGES

Set back a little from the main road to Rickmansworth, just beyond the entrance to Chessfield Park, is a row of old cottages now converted into four attractive houses. It has sometimes been alleged that they are the oldest buildings in the village, and it was once reported that they had been demolished! However, in researching the history of the Roman Villa at Latimer, the Chess Valley Archaeological and Historical Society[7] discovered a paper dealing with the ownership of Dell Farm, which is nowadays referred to as 'Latimer Park Farm'. This document records:

> In 1802 a professional survey was made. Dell Farm was described as a very ordinary farmhouse, with a granary, three barns, two stables, a cowhouse and pigsties of old construction, timber and tile, with a suckling house

> thatched. The surveyors add 'the distant part of this farm is very high and poor land, but the part nearest the homestall is some of the best land on the estate and extremely well managed'. The plan shows all the fields as they had been for at least two centuries, but a further note adds that Benjamin Lucas is the lessee for ninety nine years of certain lands on the farm from February 1796 'whereon is a newly erected cottage of brick and tile with a blacksmith's shop adjoining the Amersham Road, having a suckling house thatched and also a yard and garden'. It is concluded that the coming of the Turnpike Road from Hatfield to Reading had produced enough work to warrant such a venture.

The lease mentioned above was agreed on 12th February 1796 at five shillings per annum. Today the buildings are known as The Sheephouses. Old maps including the Tithe Map show a definite track or road running from the main road along the side of the Sheephouses, through what is now Chessfield Park down towards the lower road near Dell Farm. This track was once known as Sperlins Lane or Sperlins Plat. On the estate plan mentioned above, it bends towards the east along the top of the woods at the edge of the playing field, and then on across Stony Lane towards Chenies Manor. This latter section was once known as Ladies Walk, and John Mead states that remnants of kerbstones are still to be found there. Perhaps there was a roadway which predates the Turnpike Road of 1768.

The Sheephouses themselves are said to have been used for many decades as an overnight stopping place for sheep and cattle drovers on their way to and from the London markets. The Tithe map of 1839 shows a field called Calves Crate opposite the cottages, and this may well indicate an overnight pasture. Mr. Baldwin, an old resident who used to farm land at Martin's Top at Chenies, recalled that farmers held a regular sale of sheep, just down the slope from the Sheephouses, near the present Bedford Avenue. This would have been during the first twenty years of this century.

SNELLS FARM

The first mention of this farm is contained in the will of Samuel Snell dated 20th September 1684, in which a charge of five pounds a year was made on the estate called Snells, 'for putting out Poor Boys Apprentices whose parents were or should be inhabitants of Agmondesham'. This later became known as The Nathaniel Snell Charity. In 1858 half of the estate, including woods as far as Burtons Lane and the brick kilns, were sold to Margaret Mair, and this entailed apportioning the annual charity payment.[8] In 1912, the land was described as 'part of Snells Farm or Auntie's Property' on part of which Nightingales Cottage had been built. In 1924, the then owner Algernon Haden, living in the City of Orlando, Florida, sold about thirty-five acres to Charles Mead of Nightingales Farm, for £16,300, on condition that no house should be erected of less value than £1,000. A later restriction concerning Burtons Way stipulated that no 'hospital, church, chapel or licensed house of any description shall be erected on the said land'. The built-up area between Burtons Lane and Cokes Lane, including Burtons Way and Nightingales Corner now occupies much of this land.

LOUDHAMS FARM

This farm is shown on several maps from 1735 onwards, on one of which the name is spelt Lowdums. Little is known of earlier times, but Mrs. Nancy Thomas came across a record stating that in about 1646, the occupier was a tax collector for Charles the First named Thomas Russell, who was captured by Prince Rupert's army during the Civil War. King Charles is recorded as staying at Latimer at some stage during this troubled time. In 1820, the farm with some 85 acres was sold to Lord Henry Cavendish for £3811 by William Greening Martin of East Moulsey in Surrey.[9] Included in the property was a small dwelling called "Little Lowdhams", which may have been part of the pair of old cottages which stood on the corner of Burtons Lane until the late 1960s. In 1894 the farm was sold to the Duke of Bedford; at that time, it included all the land between the main road and the railway line from the station to the Black Horse Bridge. Twenty-six years later, in July 1920, the farm, with just eight and a half acres, was sold at public auction to Mr. Grover, the tenant, for £2,600. The rest of the land was sold off in various lots for building development.

Three other old dwellings are worth mentioning. The Piece, which lies behind the White Lion Inn, dates possibly from Elizabethan times. It has two old baking ovens, and the bedroom ceilings contain many exposed beams made from branches cut from trees. The use of such simple twisted beams are said to date the building before 1600. It has been claimed that, before the White Lion Public House was built, the Piece was itself an Inn. However, no evidence of this has been found, nor have the present owners discovered any such connection. During the last few years, the house has been lovingly restored by the owners, and is a veritable treasure.

Another house is at Beel House Nurseries in Snells Lane, where the owners, Mona and George Hance, have also carried out careful restorations. During this work, a wooden partition believed to be an Elizabethan window was uncovered between a room and an outhouse; the purpose of this window was to allow the cattle to be fed from the house, and for the room to be warmed by the heat generated by the animals. A wall painting dated about 1730 was also found behind several layers of plaster and old wallpaper, and in the same room, hidden behind more recent fireplaces, is an old inglenook which incorporated a salt oven.

The third house is Bottle Cottage in Finch Lane, which it is thought was built between 1760 and 1800. Before the road to Chalfont St. Giles through Beel Estate was closed, the house stood on a triangle of land with the road going either side of it. For many years it was used as a blacksmiths shop, and the Tithe Map of 1839[10] shows Mrs. Harriet Ayres as the owner and occupier; it has been suggested that she was herself the smith. George Ayres is shown on the 1861 census also as a blacksmith. The present owner, Mr. O'Curry, has found in the garden a considerable number of "cattle" and "pony" shoes, which are much smaller than normal horseshoes. He believes that cattle drovers used to bring herds of animals along "green lanes" to a point adjacent to a main road, where they would be shod to protect their feet on the hard road surface as they were taken to markets in London. Since the iron shoes were quite valuable, they would be removed at the market and returned to the smithy. The bottles built into the outside walls are thought to be original, and according to the County Council there are only three such cottages still standing in the county, of which the one in Finch Lane is the best example. Around the turn of the century, a policeman lived there, and across the lane was a "pound" for stray animals.

The Sheep Houses, dating from 1796, were originally built as a Smithy on the Turnpike Road.

Loudhams Barn in Burtons Lane.

Beel House Nurseries in Snells Lane, parts of which are thought to have been built by 1600.

Mrs. Harriet Bowler, the chimney sweep's wife, taken in Finch Lane complete with bird cage.

Bottle Cottage in Finch Lane is pictured on the right.

The old Post Office on Amersham Common in about 1910.

The White Lion Inn, about 1910, with Turnpike Mile Post just beyond.

The Turnpike Road

Nowadays we are all too aware of the amount of traffic which passes through the village from dawn to dusk, and even later, every day. Following the opening of the M25 motorway, more and more cars and lorries have found it convenient to converge onto the main road, and it is a frequent occurrence for traffic queues to build up solidly from the Chorleywood side by Stony Lane, all the way to the White Lion Inn and beyond. There has recently been a suggestion that the route should be turned into a 'priority road', which would almost certainly result in yet another increase in usage. But it was not always so, and the story of the road goes back several centuries.

In Roman times a network of excellent roads, with well-maintained stone surfaces, was built to facilitate the transport of goods and the movement of soldiers. Responsibility for upkeep was well-defined, and for some four hundred years the network survived. Even today, many of these roads still exist. During the dark ages after the departure of the Romans, however, the highway system fell into complete disrepair, and it was not until 1555 that a Royal Act[11] was issued placing on local parishes the responsibility for the upkeep of all roads within their boundaries. This meant, in effect, that local landowners and residents had to foot the bill, and it is hardly surprising that they were less than enthusiastic in carrying these new burdens. They saw no merit in spending good money for the benefit of others who merely passed through their parish, bringing no trade to it. The roads continued to deteriorate.

A century or so later, a new concept for repairing the highways was proposed which involved the creation of Turnpike Trusts. Today we would describe it as a form of road privatisation! A group of gentlemen, clergy, magistrates and landowners, acting as sponsors, would petition Parliament for permission to take over certain sections of the highway in order to restore and repair them. In return for providing the funds for the work to be carried out, the sponsors would be allowed to charge tolls for the passage, for example, of carriages, carts, animals and goods. The first such Act of Parliament authorising a Turnpike Trust was passed in the fifteenth year of Charles the Second's reign in 1675, covering parts of the Great North Road. Another two decades were to elapse before the experiment was repeated, but it was then so successful that numerous others were set up throughout the country. According to one survey in 1825, there were 1119 separate Trusts then in existence operating 4871 Toll Gates, and these had required 3783 individual Parliamentary Acts. Each Act was valid for only 21 years, and the theory was that, after this period, the roads in question would be handed back to the parish in good condition. In practice, however, this rarely happened, the Trustees simply reapplying for a new Act. As an illustration of the financial attractions of Turnpikes, another source (Turnpikes and Toll Booths - Seale) states that in 1821 the total annual income from all Turnpikes was £1,088,767, with an average return of £52 per mile of road.

A story often related, although the source is not known, is that

Lord Salisbury of Hatfield House in Hertfordshire suffered badly from gout. Every year in the social season, therefore, he travelled to Bath or Cheltenham in order to take the spa waters. The only route then available was via London and the Great West Road, but this was dangerous due to the attentions of highwaymen and there was also the risk of contracting disease when staying overnight at roadside inns. So the idea was mooted of building a Turnpike Road direct from Hatfield to Reading to enable him to travel much of the way in comfort and safety. The story goes on to relate how, in order to ease the torment of the gout, he would ride in his carriage with the affected leg hanging out of the window and supported on a cushion. Be that as it may, we know that a petition was presented to Parliament on 16th January 1768 (House of Commons Journals) on behalf of over five hundred gentlemen, clergy and freeholders, whose names were all listed, stating:

> ...that the road from St. Albans (via Rickmansworth, Chorleywood, Chenies, Amersham Common and Amersham) to Reading, is in a ruinous condition, and in many places extremely narrow, and that the same cannot be repaired and widened by the ordinary course of Law, and therefore preying that leave may be given to bring a Bill for repair, amend, alter, widen, turn and shorten the said several roads.

This petition was referred to a Committee which included all the MPs from Berkshire, Oxfordshire, Buckinghamshire and Hertfordshire. The resulting Act[12] (8 GEO III C.50) seems to have had an easy passage through both Houses; in the Lords, it was dealt with by a committee headed by Lord Delamer, and was dispensed with one morning before being placed that same day on the agenda for the Third Reading. The Bill received Royal Assent on March 17th 1768.

Several local dignitaries were listed in the Act, including the Drake and Lowndes families, Richard Cavendish, the Mason family from Beel House, and Coulson Scottowe of Chesham. The first meeting of the Trustees was to be held 'at the house of Mistress Warwicker known by the Sign of the Red Lion in the Borough of Chipping Wycombe'. The trustees were allowed to set up one or more turnpikes or gates across the roads, and to provide a tollhouse to each said turnpike or gate. According to the Act, tolls which could be demanded were:

> For every Horse or other Beast drawing any Waggon, Wain, Cart or other Carriage the sum of Threepence.
>
> For every Horse, Mare, Gelding, Mule or Ass, laden or unladen, and not drawing, the sum of One Penny.

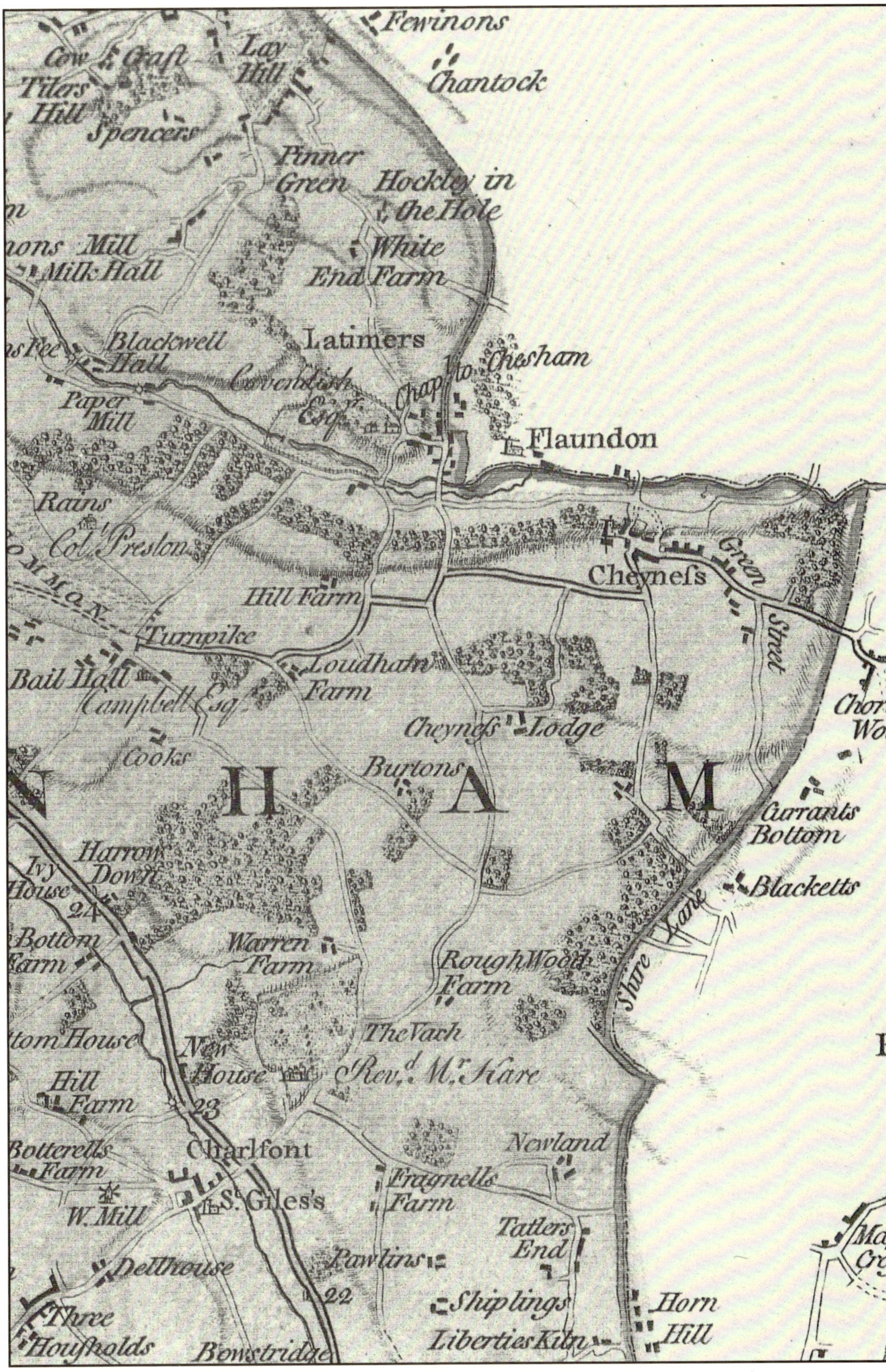

A section of Thomas Jefferys 1770 map of Buckinghamshire showing the Turnpike Gate.

> For every Drove of Oxen, Cows, or other Neat Cattle, the sum of Ten-pence per score; and so in proportion for any greater or less Number.
>
> And for every Drove of Calves, Hogs, Sheep, or Lambs, the sum of Five-pence per score; and so in proportion for any greater or less Number.

However, tolls were not to be demanded of any person who passed through the turnpike 'to and from Church, Chapel or other...Places of religious Worship on Sundays'. No dues could be asked 'for any Post-horse carrying the Mail or Packet; nor for the Horses of Soldiers passing who are upon their March...nor for Felons committed or sent to Gaol'. No tolls could be levied for passengers on horseback or in carriages for the days on which elections for Parliament took place.

Materials for making and repairing the road could be taken free of charge from adjacent land. The Trustees could appoint contractors to operate the gates and collect the tolls; indeed it was common practice for advertisements to be placed in local papers inviting tenders for this work.

The Hatfield to Reading Turnpike must have been commissioned quickly, because the 1770 map of Buckinghamshire published by Thomas Jefferys[13] shows a turnpike gate across the road at the point where Beel Lodge now stands, about 100 yards from the White Lion Inn. Confirmation of the Turnpike route is given on the strip maps issued by J. Cary in 1790.[14] This type of map was designed as a traveller's guide, each sheet being used as the journey progressed, in much the same way as motoring guides are used today. Apart from the road itself, the maps show the location of inns along the way, and landmarks such as important houses. The 1790 map shows toll gates near Cassiobury Park in Watford, at Chorleywood and next to 'Bail Hall' at the start of Amersham Common. Gates were subsequently built at Whielden Street in Amersham, and at Terriers on the road to High Wycombe.

Cary's map also shows the position of mile posts, giving the distances to both Hatfield and Reading, which are 50 miles apart. Only a few of these old posts remain, but we are fortunate in having one in Little Chalfont on the broad sweep of grass opposite the Sheephouses. It is in good condition and shows 21 miles to Hatfield, 29 to Reading, 3 to Amersham and 5 to Rickmansworth. Another post survives on the south side of the main road one mile further on towards Chenies. These posts are of cast iron, are triangular in shape, and were made by John Wilder and Sons in Reading in 1822. The firm was still in business a few years ago.

Although many old Turnpike records are held in various County Record Offices, those relating to the Hatfield - Reading one have not yet been unearthed and nothing is known about the first fifty years. In 1822, however, an

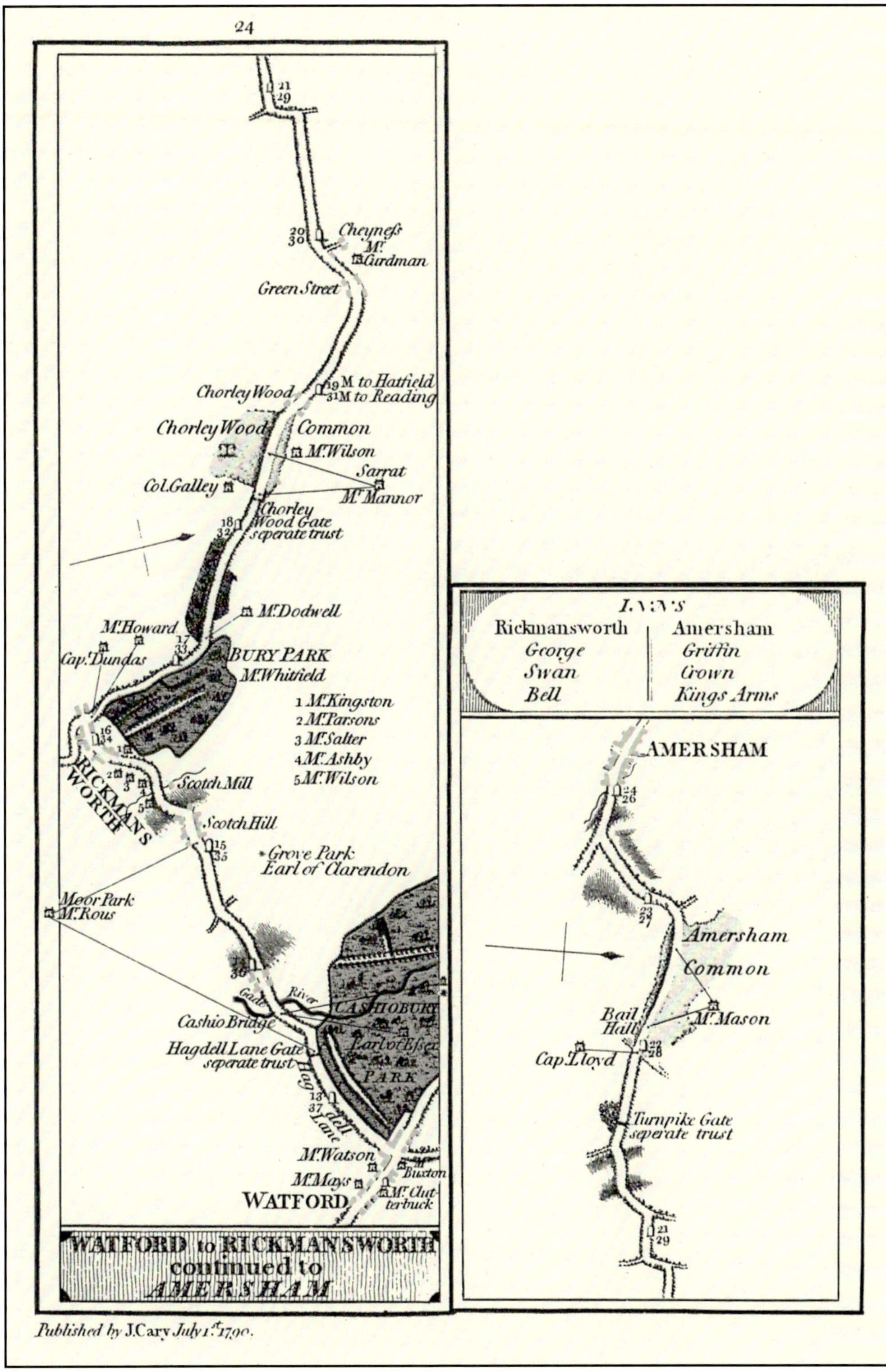

John Cary's strip map of 1790 showing the Turnpike Gate.

Act was passed (3 GEO IV C.126)[12] requiring annual accounts of all Trusts to be sent to the County Clerk of the Peace, and copies of financial statements for this Turnpike, from 1822 to 1859, are held in the Berkshire Record Office at Reading. It is somewhat surprising to find that in the year to October 1824, the income for this road amounted to £2258 9s. 9d., a considerable sum in those days. Virtually all the income was derived from the ten toll gates listed, thus giving an average of about £225 per gate. Most of the expenditure was on road repairs, and for building bridges, gates and houses. Salaries were paid to three surveyors, clerks and the treasurer. Outstanding loans amounted to £7500, and interest at 4% was paid. Clearly the road was proving a success, for by 1830 the income had risen to £3896 19s. 2d.

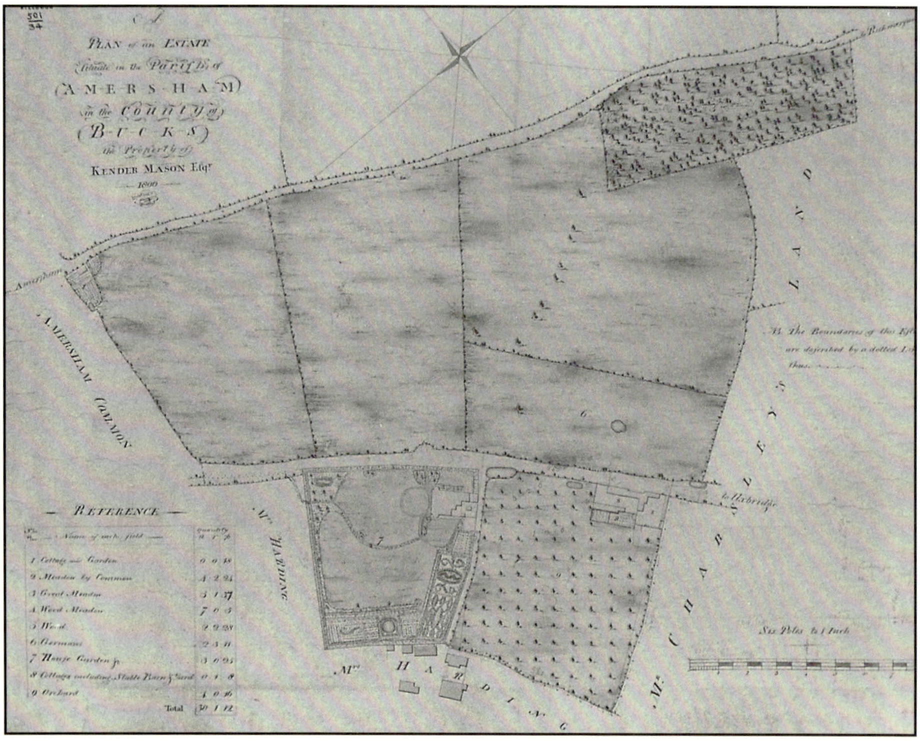

Plan of Beel House Estate 1800.

The question must now be raised whether there was a Toll House near to the present White Lion public house, and indeed whether Beel Lodge itself was the building. Both maps mentioned show a gate at this point, and an old estate map[15] of Beel House, dated 1800, shows a cottage and gardens at the spot occupied by the Lodge. Since the toll collector needed to be in attendance every day of the year from daybreak to late evening, some protection from the weather would have been needed. It is known that there were Toll Houses at the next places on the road towards Hatfield, namely at Chorleywood and also that by 1830 houses were erected at Whielden Street in Amersham and Terriers near Hazlemere. It would be strange indeed if, exceptionally, no house was provided at the spot marked near Beel House. Part of Beel Lodge still exhibits octagonal walls typical of Toll House construction, and there is evidence that the original entrance door opened directly onto the road. A surveyor's report[16] in 1961 suggests that the house could date from the 18th century. The author believes that Beel Lodge is indeed the old Toll House, and that a change occurred prior to 1820 which rendered it redundant.

Amersham Common was then an extensive stretch of open land running through Chesham Bois almost as far as Hyde Heath. An old sketch map of 1816 shows that the Common ended, not at Finch Lane and Bell Lane, but at a point some 100 yards to the east: that is, towards Rickmansworth. An earlier map by John Rocque, who was described as "Chorographer to His Royal Highness the Prince of Wales', dated 1763, shows Amersham Common criss-crossed by several tracks and lanes. The point where these converged to meet the new Turnpike Road would seem the natural spot at which to locate a Toll House. From the mid-17th century onwards, enclosure of common land became widespread, as a way of improving the fertility of the soil, and hence the size of the harvest. Under the open field system which served for hundreds of years, each small holder depended to a great extent upon his neighbours. There were virtually no fences or clear divisions between the holdings, and it was vital that farmers agreed with each other about the timing of sowing and harvesting. For example, when the need to rotate crops became better understood, difficulties arose as to who would grow wheat, and who grass. Agricultural reforms, which were badly needed in order to increase food production for the growing population, were seriously impeded by the old open system. So the movement to enclose common land and create larger workable fields was started, and local landowners started to petition Parliament for permission to enclose nearby commons. The plots of land created by the Enclosure Acts were known as Enclosure Awards or Allotments.

In the case of Amersham Common,[17] plans were drawn up in 1815, showing six enclosures along the north side of the Turnpike Road between Bell Lane and a point opposite the Pineapple Inn. Kender Mason, the owner of Beel House, was allotted one of these strips, plus two others lying to the east of Bell Lane. The result of the enclosures was that the Turnpike Road no longer opened out onto numerous tracks at the edge of the common, but simply carried straight ahead towards Amersham, with fences or hedges on either side. At the same time Kender Mason obtained permission to close part of the road which then ran from Finch Lane through his park, along Snells Lane (then called Chesham Lane) on its way towards Chalfont St Giles. It is supposed that the Trustees, finding it unprofitable to collect tolls on a straight section of road, decided to sell off the Toll House. Hence it is thought highly likely that part of the present Lodge is, in fact, the old collecting house.

With the coming of the railways, the heyday of the turnpike system passed. Traffic declined throughout the country and with it the income from tolls. During Queen Victoria's reign, virtually all Turnpike Trusts ceased to operate, and local authorities became responsible for the highways. In August 1881, a notice was issued by the Clerk to the Hatfield-Reading Trust referring to the forthcoming closure:

> Neither I nor the Trustees have received any notice from the Highway Authorities that any parts of the respective sites of the Toll Houses are required to be thrown into the Road...I, the undersigned Robert Arthur Ward, of Maidenhead, Solicitor, and Clerk to the Trustees do hereby give you notice
>
> That the Trust...will expire on the 7th day of November 1881.
>
> That it is the intention of the said Trustees to sell and convey at the expiration of the said Trust, all the Toll Houses, Gardens, and Premises adjoining the several Turnpike Gates.

Thus the Turnpike Road lasted from 1768 to 1881, a total of 113 years. Even so, the name lingered on for many years. Pam Appleby, who lives in Amersham, remembers as a small child being taken out on Sunday evenings for walks to the 'old turnpike' at Whielden Street just outside the town.

Mention has been made of stopping up the road which used to run from Finch Lane through Beel House Park on its way towards Chalfont St Giles and then to Uxbridge. This was then called Chesham Lane, and it is interesting to note that the present lane which goes past the Chalfont Colony on its way to St. Peters is also called Chesham Lane. Perhaps they were both part of an old route from Chesham to Uxbridge via the open land of Amersham Common.

Before the closure of the lane past Beel House, there was no other way of travelling from the Turnpike to St. Giles when coming from the Amersham direction. Kender Mason therefore asked the Enclosure Commissioners to create a link road from what is now Nightingales Corner to the end of Snells Lane. This explains why this stretch of road is perfectly straight, whereas most other local roads have bends and twists.

The only other straight piece on the main road is the section of Amersham Road from the end of Church Grove to Stony Lane. This, however, was constructed only in the mid-1920s. Before that, the old road used to swing along Church Grove, bending left at the junction with Lodge Lane before turning right onto the road to Chenies. Perhaps the only part of the original

Turnpike Road which gives some idea of its narrowness is the first 100 yards or so along Church Grove. The short section of hedge here is thought to be the original highway boundary.

Bell Lane, which runs from the main road down to the Chess valley, is said to have taken its name from Beel House. Beel seems to be a corruption of Bail, and the house is indeed called Bail Hall on early maps. The title deeds of one house refer to is as 'Wooden Bell Lane'. This might be a contraction of 'Wood End Bell Lane': the lane which went from the end of the woods in the valley to Bail Hall at the top of the hill. Although Finch Lane is clearly named on the Rocque map of 1763, Burtons Lane is shown as Loudhams Lane. The Tithe map of 1839 unfortunately does not give any name, and it is not known when the change took place.

Beel Lodge, 1993 - probably built before 1800 as a Toll House on the Turnpike Road.

Walking from Burtons Lane corner towards the station in 1925.
Oxford Stores and the Rendezvous can be seen with the station buildings beyond.
Banks and hedges line the road, which is un-made.

View taken in 1993.

Nightingales Corner was part of Dell Wood in 1925.
Cokes Lane is on the right with Burtons Lane at the side of the cottages.

View taken in 1993

The junction of Cokes Lane and the White Lion Road in 1925, with signpost to "The Chalfonts".

View taken in 1993.

View from Nightingales Corner along the White Lion Road towards Amersham, with Snells Wood on the left in 1925.

View taken in 1993.

Walking towards the White Lion Inn in 1925, showing the first houses to be built on the right.

View taken in 1993.

A view towards Nightingales Corner in 1925. Amersham International is now on the right and the shopping parade on the left.

View taken in 1993.

The White Lion Road near St. Nicholas Close looking towards the Village in 1925.

View taken in 1993.

The Tithe Map

A fruitful source of information for researchers is the Townsend series of Tithe Maps published in 1838. They were commissioned in an attempt to regularise the system of paying church tithes which had become, over the course of centuries, complex and difficult to control. In 1836 the Tithe Commutation Act was passed, aiming to generalise such payments. The maps which were produced are very detailed, in that every field and house is shown and numbered, and accompanying shedules list the owners, the occupiers and the sizes of each property.

The tithe system was a custom dating back to Biblical times, whereby lay people paid a levy amounting to one-tenth of their income to the church for its upkeep. Many of the magnificent cathedrals throughout Europe were financed by this method. Tithes were levied on things that 'yielded a yearly increase by the act of God', and they became mandatory in England by the tenth century. 'Praedial' tithes were payable on things arising from the ground such as grain, hay, and wood. 'Mixed' tithes were for things nourished from the ground, such as horses, lambs and hens. 'Personal' tithes were payable on profits arising from human labour and industry, such as fishing and mill operations. Some items were exempt, however, such as coal, minerals, wild deer, tame fish, or forests held by the King. Payment was usually made in kind: so many bags of corn, or so many head of cattle.

Over the years, a custom became accepted whereby the church would accept a fixed sum of money or a yearly corn rent, in place of the actual tithe. But before the Commutation Act, there was no universal method for assessing the tithe. Under the new system, Commissioners fixed the tithe income required from each parish, either by agreement or by compulsory award, and the total was then divided between the tithable land and property in that parish. Opposition against tithes gradually grew, and the system was abolished, first in Ireland in 1871, and finally in England in 1936. An indication of the resentment felt by commoners is given by this ditty, which comes from papers dealing with Grimsdell's Tomb:

> Lord save us from this thieving priest
> Who steals our crops and seize our sheep

Looking at modern ordnance survey maps of Little Chalfont can be somewhat tedious, in that the centre of the village is at the intersection of both horizontal and vertical grid lines, and one needs to look at all four adjacent sheets. A similar difficulty arises with the Tithe maps, since they were produced parish by parish, and we are at the intersection of three. The parishes of Amersham, Chenies and Chalfont St. Giles met approximately at the site of Amersham International's headquarters (Grid Ref: SU 994 976). Just to add a further problem, the scales to which they are drawn are not consistent

Several of the place names on the 1838 map are still in use today, although, not surprisingly, most of the field names have been dropped. Existing farmhouses such as Reynes (Raans), Bendrose, Cokes, Loudhams, Snells and Burtons are well marked, as well as two lesser-known ones. Colemans Farm, located in Bell Lane just to the east of the railwaly bridge, was shown on estate maps before the enclosure of the Common in 1815, and was included in the 1861 cencus. It is virtually certain that it was demolished to make way for the Metropolitan Line. Also shown, in what is now Chenies Avenue, is Old House Farm (formerly Hill Farm); access to this was not from the Turnpike Road, but from a track leading to the bottom road near Dell Farm. The farmhouse is still standing.

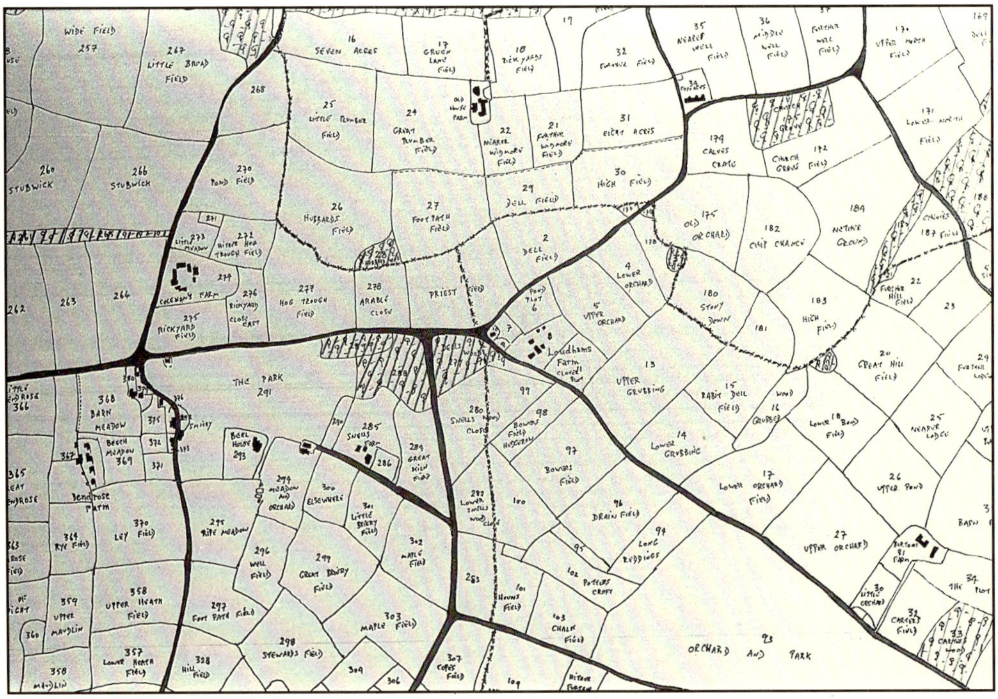

Tithe map of 1838.

Several woods appear on the map: Snells Wood, originally called Dells Wood, covers not only the present area behind the Village Hall and Library, but also the whole of Nightingale's Corner between Cokes and Burtons Lanes. This latter piece of the wood was cut off when the straight stretch of Cokes Lane was constructed in about 1820. Old photographs taken in the mid-twenties show the corner as being well wooded, and the trees were only cut down when shops were built there in 1930. Also shown on the Tithe and earlier maps, is the strip of wood which runs from Bell Lane past the timber yard towards Raans Farm, called at that time Stubwick Hedgerow. It is therefore at least two hundred and fifty years old. Church Grove takes its name from a small wood of that name and it is also shown on earlier maps. Burtons Wood on the side of Burtons Lane was called Carter's Wood on the Tithe Map.

Very few buildings, apart from the farms, are shown on the map: the Sheep Cottages, Loudhams Cottages at the corner of Burtons Lane, Beel Lodge, Beel House Nurseries in Snells Lane, and some ten cottages in Finch Lane are the only ones. The cluster in Finch Lane comprised a smithy, cottages with gardens, and a house with an orchard. The occupants listed include well-known local names such as Hance, Gomme, Mead and Baldwin.

Field names reflected the predominantly agricultural way of life; some describe straightforward features, as in Primrose Field, Great Fox Holes, Rabbit Dell, Drain Field and Hither Hog Field, while Stony Down and Maudlin draw attention to poor soil. Home Fields are almost always close to the farmhouse, and Broad Field indicated a long strip, particularly on open common ground. Lea, Lee and Ley refer to cultivated fields under grass or clover. Isle of Wight and Elsewhere indicate that these fields were remote from the farm. Fields called 'eight acre' or 'twelve acre' did not usually reflect their sizes, rather the reverse. For example, the smallest one in St. Giles' parish was called 'thousand acres'.

Names which have survived are now mostly associated with roads, such as Doggetts, Maplefield and Nightingales. A curious pair near Cokes Farm, called Burying Ground and Chapel Field, seem to indicate a religious connection; Grimsdell's Tomb lies close by, but nothing has yet been discovered about a chapel. In the centre of the village near the green, the fields were called Pond Plot, Upper, Lower and Old Orchard, and next to the telephone exchange the field was called Priests End, indicating the field furthest from the parish church in Amersham.

Brickmaking has been long established in the Chilterns,[18] and to this day bricks are still produced around Chesham. Suitable clay is readily available just a few feet below the surface, and many deep hollows can be found in the district indicating old workings. The clay was referred to as 'pug', and the children of a brickmaking family would often be given the task of turning it into a suitable state by running barefoot on the mixture; hence they were called 'puggers'. As long ago as 1774, a brick kiln was in operation in one of the fields belonging to Snells Farm. It was then let to John Ayres at a rent of eight pounds a year. Following him were William Andrew in 1830, Thomas Andrew and Company in 1842, John Andrew in 1853 and finally H Smith from 1883 to 1903 when production stopped. The census of 1851 records that Thomas Andrew and his sister Elizabeth employed seven men and a boy. Today, all that remains of the old workings are the hollows at the side of the drive leading to Dr. Challoner's High School for Girls adjacent to Snells Wood Court.

Selling beer was a common occupation, and at the end of the nineteenth century, half a dozen beer shops were listed at Amersham Common, and the Pineapple Public House was shown as such in 1851. It is thought that its name is derived from the Pomeroy family whose crest includes a pineapple. The Mason and Pomeroy families at Beel House owned plantations in the West Indies, and Beel House has a number of stone pineapples placed on the roof parapets. Perhaps 'pineapple' is a pun on 'Pomeroy'.

The White Lion Inn is recorded in a trade directory of 1830,[19] and in 1851 was being run by Samuel Wilson who was described as a 'farmer and victualer'. It is believed that the front of the inn, which is covered by a flat roof, was built as an extension to house men working on the new railway line in 1888. A local resident, Charles Bovingdon, remembers finding a plaster replica of a white lion in the front wall, when carrying out repairs to the roof in the 1950s.

Loudhams Barn in Burtons Lane.

The main road from Chenies towards Little Chalfont in 1925.

Beel Lodge in the 1930s; the road is clear of traffic.

"The Piece" is probably the oldest dwelling in the Village.

An upstairs room at "The Piece", showing crooked beams and rafters, which are said to date before 1600.

The Metropolitan Railway Line

In modern times, the Metropolitan line provides an all-electric but rather bumpy service from Amersham via Baker Street to the City. The running track is sadly in need of improvement, and the 1961 silver carriages leave much to be desired. However, plans are in preparation for a new high speed line, running from Shenstone in the east, to Aylesbury in the west, with a separate branch to Reading. Under these proposals, known as 'CrossRail', the Met will no longer serve beyond Moor Park, and after some 110 years, Little Chalfont will lose its original passenger line. If the Bill is passed by Parliament, and financial backing is found, the village may embark upon the new millennium with a transport system which provides some of the comforts enjoyed by our Victorian ancestors.

The line derived its name from the Metropolitan Railway Company, which from the 1870s onwards aimed to become the premier railway in the country, to the extent of even outstripping the Great Western and the London North East. The original part of the line ran from Baker Street to Farringdon Road, and was steam-operated. Gradually the Company extended the line, reaching Willesden Green in 1879, Harrow in 1880 and Rickmansworth in 1887. By 1889, stations had been built at Chorleywood, Chalfont Road and at Chesham, and in 1892 the route to Aylesbury was opened. The Company had ambitious plans to continue the line to the Midlands, and eventually to Scotland. They also entertained ideas of crossing London with a service to the south coast linking with cross-channel ferries. Some of these plans were realised, but the overall network was never achieved.

In order to authorise the construction of the various sections of the line, separate Acts of Parliament were required. In 1881, the Aylesbury and Rickmansworth Railway Bill was debated by a House of Commons committee.[20] Alternative routes had already been proposed, one by the LNER for a line from Watford to Chesham, and another by the GWR from Uxbridge to Amersham via the Misbourne valley. During the committee hearings, local landowners and magistrates emphasised the growing need for a new service in order to take food produce to London, and to move 'gravel and manure'. One witness stated that a new line was essential, because "the district has been more or less locked up and left, as it were, quite passive in the way of business". Another said that if he wanted to get from Chenies to Aylesbury, he would have to drive four miles to Rickmansworth, and then take a second coach 29 miles to Aylesbury, making a total of 33 miles. The Vicar of Amersham talked about the difficulties and discomforts of carrier's carts to Aylesbury, the expense of coal distribution and the problems with the flint trade for roadworks.

Once the extension to Chesham had been sanctioned, the Company started negotiations with local landowners for the purchase of land. One such agreement[21] related to the purchase of 28 acres from the Duke of Bedford at the rate of one hundred pounds per acre, amounting altogether to £2842.10s. This land was required for the station at Chalfont, and for part of the line. The document states that the Company would provide a station for passengers and goods at the Turnpike Road in Chalfont St. Giles (sic), and a properly constructed access road twenty feet wide not exceeding 1 in 20 gradient. Also four bridges each fourteen feet wide (presumably those at Lodge Lane, behind Oakington Avenue, the main road near the station and at Bell Lane), and all necessary fencing to the Duke's land.

While the station was being built in 1888, discussion centred around a suitable name for it. It is worth recalling that, at this time, there were virtually no houses here, and also that the Chalfont St. Giles parish boundary reached as far as the present Bedford Avenue. Residents of St. Giles therefore regarded the new station as theirs. The following letter[22] from the Rector of St. Giles, the Revd. Downall W Phipps, dated 22nd November 1888, suggested a name linked to the parish:

> To the Board of the Metropolitan Railway —
> I am requested by some of the chief residents and owners in this neighbourhood, to convey to you the expression of their earnest hope that the new station in this parish may be named **CHALFONT ROAD.**
>
> As the station will be used by the two parishes named Chalfont, and will attract to itself the custom of the Chalfont neighbourhood, I am confident you will see the importance of giving it the name of Chalfont.
> One great advantage to us which your line we hope will afford, will be to set us free from the difficulty which at present is a great annoyance of having to explain why our railway station is Uxbridge and not Slough, which is the Post Town. But if you call our station by any other name than Chalfont, you will leave us as badly off as ever.
>
> Whilst writing on the subject, may I also ask whether you could provide a footpath at any rate, from the station from the down platform across the field straight to our road, to relieve us from the necessity of going round nearly a quarter of a mile, with a very steep hill, to enter the station.

The latter remark refers to a problem which lasted a further forty years after the station opened, in that the sole entrance and exit was on the London or up side. It was only in 1927 that a footpath was opened on the village side, leading to the steps down to the main road, and across to Village Way. The roadway called 'Station Approach' was not created until 1933. Thus in the early years passengers leaving the station had to walk down the far approach road, under the bridge and along a narrow country lane to the junction with Burtons Lane. The message on the back of a postcard of 1910 illustrates the point. It was from Freda and Jules at Hill Cottage, Amersham Common:

> Dear Harry,
> Yours to hand. Glad to see you with songs. If you care to come on Sunday morn and stay till Monday. For an excursion ticket (weekend) it is cheaper. Turn right on leaving the station door, turn right under arch and then along the White Lion Road, following the rail line as if you had continued in train. Our cottage, now 'Hill Cottage', is at the end of the village, a few steps after P.O. If you can let us know train you are coming by, we will meet you 'a la Gare'. Come to Chalfont Road Station.

The village referred to was of course Amersham Common, and since houses had not then been built along the main road, the railway line could be easily seen when walking along the road.

Chalfont Road station was officially opened on July 18th 1889, on the same day as Chesham. Since there was as yet no service to Amersham, horse-drawn coaches connected with the train schedules. A note in Kelly's Directory for 1891 announced:

> Omnibus leaves the Griffin Hotel (in Amersham) for Chalfont Road station on the Metropolitan railway at 8.20am, and 2.30, 4.30 and 6.30pm; returning from station at 10.24am and 12.24, 4.24, 6.24 and 7.24pm arriving at Amersham about 35 minutes later. Conveyance in readiness to meet all trains.
>
> Thomas William's conveyance leaves the Pheasant Inn (St. Giles) at 8.20am in connection with the fast train leaving Chalfont Road station at 8.53am, and waits till the arrival of the 9.29am from London on weekdays; also leaves the Pheasant Inn at 5.30pm weekdays and 9.30am Sundays.

Eventually the line was extended to Amersham and beyond, opening on September 1st 1892. The construction from Rickmansworth to Aylesbury involved raising the sum of £533,000. David Smith, a local resident, recalls that when the line had been completed, his father used to walk to Chesham along the track, and others have said it was quicker to walk to Rickmansworth along the line, rather than by road.

Much of the present station building is original, and the roofs at the centre of the platforms are admired for their decorative cast-iron columns and beams. Five roof sections were provided on the London side, but only three on the other, and it is quite easy to see where they were extended later. At first there was no waiting room, and travellers had to wait until 1912 for a shelter, costing £40, to be erected. A cycle shed had been put up the year before for £42.

Perhaps one of the highlights concerning the development of the Met., was the announcement in 1910 of the introduction of a Pullman Car service. In May of that year two cars, named 'Mayflower' and 'Galatea', began to run from Aylesbury to Aldgate, and continued to do so until the outbreak of war in 1939. They were fitted out in a very opulent style: one had a mahogany finish with inlaid satinwood and green upholstery, and the other had oak with crimson finish. Each table was glass-topped with an ornate lamp and a push button for service. Refreshments were served including breakfast on morning trains, and theatre suppers late in the evening. The supplement for Pullman cars was advertised as sixpence to Rickmansworth, and one shilling beyond. To celebrate the inauguration of the service, lunch was laid on at the George Hotel in Aylesbury, and there was a special train for representatives of the press. The luxury service became very popular and ran every day except Sundays. Theatre-goers were catered for by two late evening runs, the last one to Aylesbury being at midnight.

In 1915, presumably to widen the catchment area from which travellers could be drawn, Chorleywood station had Chenies added to its name, and Chalfont Road was changed to the present name of **Chalfont and Latimer.** This took place on 20th November. The Company was clearly looking forward to an increase in train commuting once the war was over.

The Company had already built up a considerable traffic in goods and minerals, by offering facilities for 'coal, coke, cement, bricks, stone, tiles and timber', as well as for 'grain, flour, oil cake, manure, groceries, farm produce and other merchandise'. Posters claimed boldly that the Met. was in communication with the railways of the London and North Western, Midland, Great Central and Great Western Companies. Articles to be sent by goods train were to be distinctly addressed 'per goods train', and it was stressed that they should be directed 'by Metropolitan Railway'. Many of the stations along the line had facilities for collecting and delivering goods by cart or van, but not Chorleywood or Chalfont Road. Between the wars, however, Chalfont and Latimer became a substantial goods centre, with two separate sidings in the space now occupied by the upper station car park. In particular, there was a large coal depot from which Darvells made deliveries to houses in the district, and also a National Benzole oil depot at the side of Bedford Avenue now taken over by the lower car park. The oil trade survived until about 1960.

As the numbers of passengers grew, complaints started to be heard about the lack of facilities at the station. Customers from Chesham, who had to change trains, as well as commuters from the residential area growing up around the station, wrote to the Company, saying that it was most inconvenient having to wait for connections, especially in winter and whenever the weather was poor. The only shelter was very small and unheated, and the platforms were open to the winds, since there were no enclosing walls or fences. A deputation was sent to present its case to the railway managers, and one of the arguments[23] used was that:

> There is a new estate under development upon which over thirty houses have been erected since last July, but progress is slow because of the inconvenience at Chalfont station. Cases have been reported where people taking up houses at Chesham have left after only three years because of the objections at Chalfont station.

This was in February 1927. Later that year oil lamps were provided on the platforms, and soon afterwards a new larger waiting room was built.

LOCAL DATA OF RESIDENTIAL DISTRICTS IN METRO-LAND.

Station.	Trains (each way) daily.	Journey time to or from Baker St.	Local Rates (in the £).	Gas per 1000 feet (a): per th'm (b).	Charge for Water.	Electric Light (per unit).	Altitude above sea level.	Subsoil.
Willesden Green	282	8 mts.	11/6	3/7 (a)	6½% rate val.	4d.	180 ft.	Clay
Neasden	222	12 ,,	9/4	3/7 (a)	5¾% ,,	4d.	127 ft.	Gravel and clay
Wembley Park	287	11 ,,	9/6	3/10 (a)	7% ,,	4d.	234 ft.	Clay
Preston Road	119	13 ,,	9/6	3/10 (a)	7% ,,	4d.	162 ft.	,,
Northwick Park & Kenton ..	131	14 ,,	9/6	3/10 (a)	7% ,,	4d.	175 ft.	,,
Harrow-on-the-Hill	193	15 ,,	7/8	3/9 (a)	6-8.4% ,,	5d.	400 ft.	,,
West Harrow	77	19 ,,	8/6	3/9 (a)	6-8.4% ,,	4½d.	196 ft.	,,
Rayners Lane (for Harrow Garden Village)	75	21 ,,	8/4	1/- (b)	6½% ,,	6½d.	175 ft.	Loamy clay
Eastcote	45	23 ,,	10/2	1/- (b)	5½-7% plus 20%	6½d.	196 ft.	,,
Ruislip	49	25 ,,	10/2	1/- (b)	5½-7% plus 20%	6½d.	168 ft.	Gravel and clay
Ickenham	44	28 ,,	11/10	1/- (b)	5% rate val.	6d.	207 ft.	,, ,,
Hillingdon	45	30 ,,	11/10	1/- (b)	5% ,,	6d.	117 ft.	,, ,,
Uxbridge	49	30 ,,	12/-	1/- (b)	1/4 in £ rate val.	6d.	200 ft.	,, ,,
North Harrow	68	19 ,,	8/5½	1/- (b)	6-8.4% ,,	6½d.	175 ft.	Clay
Pinner..	68	21 ,,	9/1	5/- (a)	6-8.4% ,,	6½d.	163-230 ft.	,,
Northwood	72	23 ,,	10/2	1/- (b)	5½-7% plus 20%	6½d.	200-450 ft.	Gravel and clay
Moor Park & Sandy Lodge ..	54	30 ,,	11/-	1/0½ (b)	5% gross val.	8d.	380 ft.	Gravel and chalk
Croxley Green	45	32 ,,	10/8	1/0½ (b)	5% ,,	8d.	350 ft.	,, ,,
Watford	47	34 ,,	11/10	9¼ (b)	1/- in £	3d.	150-350 ft.	,, ,,
Rickmansworth	46	27 ,,	11/-	1/0½ (b)	5% gross val.	8d.	150-270 ft.	,, ,,
Chorley Wood & Chenies ..	39	34 ,,	10/4	13.9d. (b)	5% rate val.	8d.	368 ft.	,, ,,
Chalfont & Latimer	40	38 ,,	10/6	1/- (b)	5⅔% ,,	7d.	410 ft.	,, ,,
Chesham	26	48 ,,	11/6	11d. (b)	10d. in £ per yr.	7d.	330-526 ft.	,, ,,
Amersham & Chesham Bois ..	32	40 ,,	10/2	1/- (b)	7½% rate val.	7d.	300-540 ft.	,, ,,
Great Missenden	28	49 ,,	10/-	1/- (b)	5⅔% ,,	7d.	400-600 ft.	,, ,,
Wendover	26	58 ,,	10/-	1/6 (b)	7½% gross val.	8d.	450-900 ft.	,, ,,
Aylesbury	27	73 ,,	13/-	1/4 (b)	6½% rate val.	8d.	275 ft.	Clay & friable rock

Local data of residential districts in Metro Land - 1932.

As a further encouragement to people to live away from London, a series of booklets was published annually from 1919 onwards by the Metropolitan Railway. The delights of living in the country were extolled, and descriptions of local attractions were given. Even in 1932, Chalfont and Latimer was listed only as a starting point for visiting Latimer and the two Chalfonts, although there is mention of a new residential quarter which would soon require a name of its own. (This was seven years after the present name had been adopted!) The Company also issued attractive booklets describing walks between stations along the line: several routes along the Chess valley and to Amersham, starting at the station, were included. These Metroland booklets convey an atmosphere of a leisured way of life, with emphasis on good clean air and open countryside. In 1932, trains took 38 minutes to Baker Street, and there were forty each way per day. A first class ticket to Liverpool Street cost nineteen shillings and threepence per week, while a third class one was twelve shillings and ninepence. Hunting in Bucks and Herts was also catered for, as described in a Metro poster:[24]

> For the convenience of Hunting Gentlemen, a train now leaves Baker Street at 9.5am. Hunters to be boxed at Finchley Road by 9.0am. For horse boxes apply to any of the stations. The fare for the horses varies from five to fifteen shillings, and for riders from two shillings and sixpence to eight shillings and nine pence.

An indication of the more relaxed way of life then is revealed in this letter[25] from one of the general managers of the railway to the Chief Engineer:

> My Dear Jack,
> Mr. Stafford of Chenies shoots some of the woods on both sides of the railway line near Chalfont Road station. He has put an extra keeper on this section with the idea of having more pheasants. He asks permission for his keepers to go on the banks to pick up eggs and keep an eye on the nests. He wishes to have your official consent. Can you manage this for him?
> PS: When I have shot with him, we stand on the line to get some good high birds. Perhaps you would sanction this at the same time.

This letter was written in 1931, and the station was still being called by its old name, even though it had been changed fifteen years earlier.

Until 1961, the trains to Chalfont were drawn by electric locomotives as far as Rickmansworth, and then by steam for stations beyond, and this entailed a four-minute wait while the engines were changed. The passenger carriages were of the old-fashioned type, with individual compartments entered from separate doors, and there were no corridors or toilets. In 1961, the present all-electric trains were brought into service, powered by ground-level conductors. For those who remember the introduction of the new silver coaches, it is hard to realise that they are now over thirty years old, and are due to be replaced.

Bridges built in the late Victorian period were meant to last. Although trains became longer, faster and heavier, the old bridges were able to carry the loads until quite recently. However, in 1975, engineers found that the one next to the station was unsafe and needed to be widened and strengthened. The replacement was fabricated mostly off-site, and the whole operation of removing the old and fitting the new was carried out during only one weekend.

The latest proposals for CrossRail involve overhead electrification at high voltage, extended platforms, longer and faster trains, and shorter travel times to certain London destinations. Parliamentary approval will be needed by 1995, if the new system is to start operating in the year 2000.

Original Victorian cast iron columns at the station.

Train arriving at Chalfont Road Station from Amersham at the turn of the century.

Postcard of about 1910 giving directions from Chalfont Road Station to Hill Cottage near the Black Horse Bridge at Amersham Common.

Taken in the 1920s, this shows the wooden sheds on the right where Munn & Chapman started their garage. There is no footpath and hedges line both sides. Houses in Village Way are on the left.

Taken in the early 1930s, this also shows the wooden sheds. Graham's Garage to the right of the bridge advertises Armstrong Siddeley cars, and self-changing gears.

Bedford Avenue and the "Mushroom Field" taken from the station approach, looking towards Chenies Avenue.

The newly constructed entrance to the station in 1934. Graham's Garage became the Station Garage in that year. Pretty and Ellis had an estate office in the wooden building on the right.

The Start of The Village

At the turn of the century, the Metropolitan Line had been in operation for just over ten years, but the station was still quite isolated with the nearest town or village some three miles away. The population of Amersham was about three thousand, and that of Amersham Common not more than one hundred and fifty. Apart from the old farmhouses referred to earlier, the only dwellings here were the Sheephouses, Loudhams Cottages, Beel House and its Lodge, about ten cottages in Finch Lane and two or three in Snells Lane. The number of people living in what we now regard as Little Chalfont was not much greater than one hundred, and this pattern did not change significantly for another twenty years or so. Mr. Haddon, who owned the chemist shop in Amersham for many years, wrote his memories of those days:

> Before the First World War, this area was known as Chalfont Road. As those lovely trains of the Metropolitan and Great Central railway pulled into the station, the porters would call out 'Chalfont Road, junction for Chesham'. From the White Lion and along by Snells Wood, a winding country road with fairly high banks surmounted by hedges made its way past Cokes Lane, an almost concealed turn, and round under the bridge and up to the Sheep Houses on the corner. It was just wide enough for two big farm waggons to pass. Wild flowers grew and birds nested in the banks and hedges. On the right hand side going from the White Lion, the only house was the lodge to Beel House which is still there today. On the other side was the yard and workshop of Grovers, Agricultural Engineers, like Boughtons but on a smaller scale. I seem to recall that they owned a Steam Foden Waggon, a Steam Roller and a Traction Engine. The next buildings were the two cottages on the corner, where our village green now is, but which was then their gardens. Where Chenies Parade now stands, was a meadow with a six foot high metal fence, with about four inch iron palings. It was part of Loudhams Farm, and the high wall behind the shops was then the wall of a lovely fruit orchard, also part of the farm. The old road ran much nearer to the meadow, but the corner has been taken off, and the new road is of course, much wider. On the other side of the station was Oldhouse farm, and looking from the train one could see a cart track leading to the farm buildings and the rickyards.

Although development of the area was destined to be delayed, the first inklings of what was to come appeared in 1894, only five years after the opening of the Metropolitan Line. A preliminary advertisement[26] in local papers announced 'Lucrative Speculation in Building Land immediately adjoining CHALFONT ROAD STATION'. One hundred and thirty-six acres of freehold land were offered for sale by Public Auction at Amersham on 6th July, by Lord Chesham. One of the attractions claimed was that it included a valuable hotel site next to the station. The land in question lay between the main road and the railway line, and extended from the station to Flack's Garage at Amersham Common. Also included was Loudhams Farm, two fields in Burtons Lane, the field behind the shopping parade, and Village Way. The Duke of Bedford, however, did not like the idea of new housing developments next to his estate on the other side of the railway; he therefore purchased all the land for £13,615, giving as his main reason:

> This property is about to be sold in lots as a building estate without restriction as to the nature or purpose of the erections - such an event, owing to its proximity to London, and the new line of the Metropolitan Railway Company, would seriously prejudice the privacy of His Grace's Chenies Estate, which (it) is most desirable to maintain, and the acquisition of it appears to be the only way of accomplishing this object.

The passage of the years, however, brought about a change of mind. On Thursday, 15th July 1920, at Hanover Square, His Grace the Duke of Bedford offered for sale by auction,[27] fourteen lots of valuable freehold land suitable for building estates. The properties, and indeed the individual plots, were those purchased twenty-six years earlier in order to prevent house building! Most of the lots were sold on the day, including Loudhams Farmhouse with eight acres, which was bought for £2600 by the sitting tenant Mr. Grover. Lot number eleven, extending to over fourteen acres and now occupied by Village Way, went for £1475. The two old cottages which used to stand on the corner of Burtons Lane, where we now have the village green, were sold at £650. They contained three and four rooms respectively, with outhouses, and were rented to Mrs. Lawrence and Mr. Hance for a total of £6.18s.8d per annum.

It was following the sale of these building sites that development of the area started to go ahead. The first houses were built by the Rural District Council in about 1921, opposite the White Lion public house on the corner of Bell Lane, and an old postcard shows the lane having a rough, un-made surface. On Amersham Common, a new 'Recreation Hall' was opened on the 9th June 1922, and, not to be outdone, Amersham opened a new cinema, concert and dance hall known as 'The Pavilion' on 24th November.

By direction of His Grace The Duke of Bedford, K.G.

Buckinghamshire Adjacent to Chalfont Road Station (On the Metropolitan & Great Central Railways).

Two miles from Amersham, and five miles from Rickmansworth, and 40 minutes by Rail from Town.

PARTICULARS, PLAN AND CONDITIONS OF SALE

OF THE

Valuable FREEHOLD Property

(being an Outlying Portion of THE CHENIES ESTATE)

FORMING PART OF

Loudhams Farm & Lodge Farm

COMPRISING

FARM DWELLING HOUSE and TWO COTTAGES,
NUMEROUS ELIGIBLE BUILDING SITES
with Extensive Main Road and Railway Frontages,

THE WHOLE EXTENDING TO ABOUT

148·731 Acres.

To be offered for Sale by Auction in Fourteen Lots by Messrs.

Knight, Frank and Rutley

(Sir Howard G. Frank, K.C.B., John Frederick Knight, Alfred J. Burrows and Arthur Horace Knight.)

At The Estate Sale Room, 20, Hanover Square, London, W.,
On THURSDAY, JULY 15th, 1920,
At 2.30 o'clock precisely (unless previously disposed of).

Solicitor :	FRED T. TANQUERAY, Esq., Woburn, Beds.	
Land Agent :	C. P. HALL, Esq., Estate Office, Woburn, Beds.	
Auctioneers :	Messrs. KNIGHT, FRANK & RUTLEY,	20, Hanover Square, W.1; 41, Bank Street, Ashford, Kent; 100, Princes Street, Edinburgh; 78, St. Vincent Street, Glasgow.

Announcement of Sale of Land from the station to the outskirts of Amersham, all part of Loudhams Farm - 1920.

Development of the centre of the village itself can be said to have commenced early in 1922, with the formation of a limited company having interests in land at **Chalfont Station Village.** The firm was named Morlands Concessions Ltd, with offices at Rickmansworth and at Little Chalfont. An article appeared in 1925, in the Westminster Illustrated magazine, describing the company as one of the most progressive in the country, and recommending it to prospective house purchasers:

> It is interesting to recall some of the history of this firm, in that it is largely a history of perseverance and hard work, first on the part of its founder, and then on the part of the Directors. The business was started in late 1921 by Mr. Howard Freeborn, B.A. who opened his office at Chalfont Station Village, and undertook as his first task the building of a thatched bungalow — work mainly carried out with his own hands. During the following year he was successful in securing a good many orders for the erection of country cottages, and the scope of the business was greatly enlarged. In November 1922, a limited company was formed.
>
> Thanks to the energy which was consistently put behind it, the business grew and prospered, and an office was opened in Rickmansworth to carry on the business of auctioneers, estate agents and surveyors. At Chalfont Station Village, they are building small detached residential properties, with water, gas, and electric light; and it is interesting to note that this estate has a height of five hundred feet above sea level, and that there is a very fine train service, both fast and frequent.

Mr. Haddon remembers speaking to the building foreman who told him that Captain Freeborn said to him one day, "Frank, we are going to put up these houses but building costs are high, and I do not know what to use for roofing. Tiles cost a small fortune." The foreman said, "Why not thatch them, sir?" They then brought an old craftsman from Oxfordshire, and that was the beginning of their thatched houses in Little Chalfont.

Meanwhile, work was started on houses along the White Lion Road between Bell Lane and Loudhams Road. One of the first, 'Markham', was built in 1925 for Mrs. Gladys Swain's father, Mr. Wood, and the builder was Fred Honour, who erected most of the other houses along the main road, including the two shops on the corner of Bell Lane. In Finch Lane, Mrs. Eliza Woolhead used to run a general store selling paraffin and other old items from the front room of her house.

Two houses, with shops below, were built about 1925 close to the station; one became the Oxford Store, which was taken over in 1928 by Dudley Rhodes' father, who then established the sub-Post Office; the other became the Rendezvous, selling confectionery, stationery and newspapers, which was run by Mrs. Bedfer. Her husband had a cycle repair business in sheds called the White Lion Garage, now the site of the petrol station opposite the Pineapple Inn. Loudhams Road was also started in 1925, by a builder named Hancock, who put up most of the detached houses; the semi-detached ones were constructed by Wheelers of Chorleywood.

After the end of the war, the Metropolitan Railway Company was anxious to increase its passenger traffic, and hence its turnover, and hit on the idea of buying up land alongside the tracks, and setting out roads for housing estates. In 1919, the Metropolitan Railway Country Estates Ltd. was formed, and announced:

Page 266 THE WESTMINSTER ILLUSTRATED.

The Design and Construction of Country Houses.

Birdseye View of Chalfont Station Village.

ONE of the most interesting businesses which we have had the pleasure of reviewing in the columns of this journal is that of Messrs. Morlands Concessions, Ltd., who have their offices at Council Chambers, Rickmansworth, and at Chalfont Station Village, Amersham, Bucks. This very interesting Company are carrying on the best of good work as surveyors, estate agents and valuers; but they are also keenly interested in the design and construction of country houses, much of their most effective work lying along these lines. The Directors have been eminently successful with country homes, and their fund of modern ideas, and the close attention which they give to all matters of detail in this important work have given them a standing in their own locality which is second to that of no other firm.

It is the more interesting to recall some of the history of this firm, in that it is largely a history of perseverance and hard work, first on the part of its founder, and then on the part of the Directors of the Company, two of whom, at least, are very keenly and actively interested in all the work undertaken.

The business was started late in 1921 by Mr. Howard Freeborn, B.A., who opened an office at Chalfont Station Village, and undertook as his first task the building of a thatched bungalow—work mainly carried out with his own hands. During the following year he was successful in securing a good many orders for the erection of country cottages, and the scope of the business was greatly enlarged. In November, 1922, a limited Company was formed, with interests in land at Chalfont Station Village, which adjoins Chalfont and Latimer Station, on the Metropolitan and G.C. Railways, and Chorleywood Estate, Loudwater.

Thanks to the energy which was consistently put behind it, the business grew and prospered, and an office was opened in Rickmansworth to carry on the business of auctioneers, estate agents and surveyors, which also has prospered and increased in a fine manner. The Directors have built between forty and fifty houses on the various estates in which they are interested, and which offer very fine facilities for country homes for those engaged in town during the day. At Chalfont Station Village they are building small detached residential property, with water, gas, and electric light; and it is interesting to note that this Estate has a height of five hundred feet

House at Chalfont Station Village.

Bungalow at Chalfont Station Village. Messrs. Morlands Concessions, Ltd.

An article in the Westminster Illustrated dated February 1925, describing the houses being built in Chalfont Station Village.

> The MRCE has been organised, not merely to provide superior houses in rural countryside near London, but also to create new passenger traffic for the railway. The Company is therefore able to do more and give more than mere rent-depending property.

In order to advertise the attractions, a slogan 'Come and Live in Metroland' was coined, and even the door handles of the train carriages carried the message. Estates were created adjacent to almost all the stations along the line, including here at Chalfont. Chenies Avenue and Beechwood Avenue were both laid out, and plots of land were offered for sale by the Company. The line of sycamore trees in Beechwood Avenue was planted in the early 1920s, and three houses were built there in the 1930s. Metro-style houses were also built in Amersham Way, and at the Lodge Lane end of Church Grove.

The Estates Company advertised houses for sale at prices between £725 and £1,100, catering for every demand: detached, semi-detached and bungalows. The publicity also contained the plan below, and mentioned that some 30 acres of land a few hundred yards from the station were being developed. It is not known why the road called Central Way in the centre of the plan was not built, nor why the name 'Chenies Estate' did not survive.

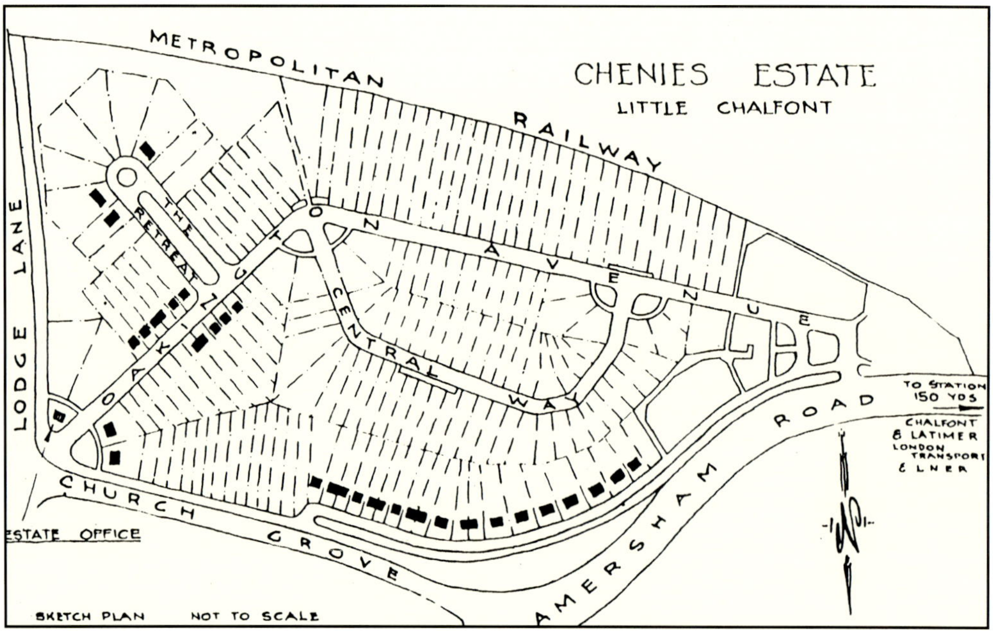

Proposed layout of Chenies Estate, Little Chalfont - 1936.

Although the Estates Company was responsible for much of the pre-War growth of the village, there is no doubt that it all started opposite the station in the present Village Way. By 1925, some thirty or so houses had been built by Captain Freeborn's company, and for a few years the development was called Chalfont Station Village, as this invitation card shows:

Mrs Michael Duparc

At home

The Bynn,
Chalfont Station Village,
(Chalfont & Latimer Station.)
Bucks.

The origin of the name **Little Chalfont** has been the subject of speculation over the years, and since it does not appear on any old maps, it clearly is an invented one. It first appears on the ordnance survey map of 1926, exactly on the area covered by the houses in Village Way. The source of the name was initially difficult to track down, since some of the Chalfont St Giles' Parish Minute Books were missing from the Records Office. In the end, however, they were recovered, and were found to contain the answer to the puzzle. A minute dated the 15th January 1925 reads:

> Proposed by Mr. Newton, seconded by Mr. Horne, "That the Council agree the request of the inhabitants of Chalfont Station Village for it to be renamed **Little Chalfont**".

The Bucks Examiner announced this decision, highlighted in a black frame somewhat like an obituary notice, in their issue of 30th January 1925:

> **We are informed that the name of Chalfont Station Village has been changed, upon the suggestion of residents and with the approval of Chalfont St. Giles Parish Council and the sanction of the Director General of the Ordnance Survey. It will in future be known as Little Chalfont.**

One mystery remains unsolved, however: Mrs. Bowler, the wife of the chimney sweep who lived in Finch Lane, recalled in 1975 that the part of the village near the green was once called 'Bunker's Green'; in addition, the parish minutes of October 1921 proposed 'that the Clerk write to the County Council calling their attention to the state of the bad corner at Bunker's Green near Chalfont Road station, trusting that they will consider the same with a view to widening the same'. No other trace of this name has yet been found, but it is interesting to speculate that when a name was being chosen for the village, Bunker's Green might have been selected!

The story has been recounted several times, by residents who lived here before the 1939 war, explaining why most of the thatched roofs in Village Way have been replaced by tiles. The railway line from Rickmansworth and Chorleywood has a steep gradient as it climbs towards the Chiltern Hills, and the steam engines had to work hard, especially when drawing long and heavy loads. If the wind was in the appropriate direction, smoke and sparks from the funnels would be carried across the road and on to Village Way. This resulted in many of the thatches being set on fire, and the volunteer fire brigade being called out from Amersham. Ivy Wheeler remembers the wife of one of the residents rushing into the greengrocer's shop at Nightingales Corner, and asking for the brigade to be summoned urgently. It has been said that Captain Freeborn's own roof was the first to suffer. One by one, over a period of ten years or so, insurance companies paid for the replacements. St. Giles Parish Minutes of 7th July 1925 report a request for fire hydrants to be provided at Little Chalfont, but the matter was 'left on the table'. One and a half years later, the council recorded that they could not entertain the idea of putting up hydrants.

At about the same time, the council was asked to provide road lights, but the Uxbridge Electrical Company said that they could not undertake the work since Village Way was privately owned. The residents replied that, although the road was private, it was used by the public, and was never closed. In the event, the council obtained written permission from residents to erect lamps. Quotations were received from Messrs. Lucy & Co. of Oxford, for the supply of three lamps at £8.50s each. It was also agreed that Mr. Percy West from Amersham Common Post Office would switch the lights on and off, for a payment of £3.3s per year. This was in February 1927. Later that year, Messrs. Anderson, Musk, Kipling and Duparc asked that the lamps should be left on until the last train at night; but the council refused, saying that the times had already been fixed for the lamps to be put out at 10.30pm, and that they could not see any reason for altering their decision.

In 1922, the County Council carried out a count of the traffic[28] using the main road from Amersham to Rickmansworth, during one week in August. Bearing in mind the amount of traffic today, the numbers are unbelievably low, perhaps only one car every three minutes or so:

Cycles	2883
Motor Vehicles	2792
Horse-Drawn Vehicles	393
Hand Carts etc.	625
Total	6693

The road, however, was then still as described by Mr. Haddon, a narrow winding lane with barely enough room for two large carts to pass. A road-widening scheme was therefore undertaken by the County Council, and a series of photographs was taken to assist the highway engineers. These give a fascinating view of the White Lion Road, especially the part which is now the village centre. The road towards the station, which can just be discerned in the distance, is unmade and flanked by hedges and trees. The corner between Cokes and Burtons Lanes is heavily wooded, and ruts appear in the road surface. The road from Nightingales Corner to the White Lion public house was increased by some ten feet in width along the side nearest to Snells Wood. According to Mrs. Swain, the widening was carried out in 1926 and involved cutting down a strip of woodland immediately adjacent to the road. Clearly the road was being opened up to permit further developments.

After the Oxford Store and the Rendezvous, the next shops to appear, at the end of 1929, were Cullen the grocer and Berkley the butcher, both at Nightingales Corner, followed within a year by Lofts the ironmonger, and Weatherill the chemist. Norman Lofts was well known and regarded affectionately as a 'character'. Nothing was too much trouble when serving a customer, one of whom remembers going into the shop for just two wood screws. After the customer had been shown all the types of screws in stock, and had selected the right ones, Norman insisted on wrapping them in a small brown paper parcel, saying that the customer didn't want to soil his hands by carrying them loose.

The original Munn and Chapman garage had already been built in 1928. By 1932, Barclays Bank had opened a part-time branch, the Sugar Loaves public house had opened, and Clifton Brothers were running an electrical shop next to Munn and Chapmans. Within a year or two, other shops opened at Nightingales Corner including the greengrocer Plummer, Lloyds Bank and the estate agent Herbert Fisk. Shops were also built round the corner opposite the present Village Hall, consisting of Bail the greengrocer, the ladies' outfitters Meadows, and Stowells wine shop.

A small wooden shed was put up in Village Way, at the top of the steps which still exist opposite the station, and opened business as the 'Cosy Café', which later became the 'Little Chalfont Café'. This café was apparently very popular, especially among shop workers, and several people have related how Mr. Bail first met the lady who was to become his wife, when she served him cups of tea! After the war, the shed became a men's hairdresser shop run by Mr. Gill.

Development of the village continued apace; the Golden Hind cake and tea rooms opposite the end of Cokes Lane were run by the Misses Bentham, and along the White Lion Road near Loudhams Road, Oakwood Gardens nursery was started by Mr. Whitaker. Caudrey the Builder, later to become Amersham Estates Ltd, took the last shop but one in Burtons Lane, and Swannell and Sly started as estate agents next to the Post Office. Gates the Builder opened next to the present telephone exchange, with Miss Constance Glaze on the floor above selling ladies' gowns. Sandwiched between them and Munn and Chapman was Ken Kipling, selling fruit, flowers and vegetables, with 'Irene' the hairdresser above. In the Station Approach, another ladies' hairdresser, 'Elaine', opened next door to the 'Opal Café' run by Miss Parks. Next to the station entrance, London Kiosks sold tobacco and sweets. On the corner of Village Way opposite the Post Office, the National Provincial Bank offered a part-time service. On the other corner of Village Way, a wooden shed housed the Reliance shoe-repairers and bootmakers. Other enterprising businesses were springing up; for example, an advertisement in January 1925 said that 'Mademoiselle Camp visits and receives pupils for French, German and English at Holne, Chalfont Station Village'. Miss Grace Harvey opened a Prep School called St. Nicholas (now the site of St. Nicholas Close).

Facing page of a pre-War greengrocer's account book.

As has been mentioned, Church Grove used to be the route of the old main road, and it was not until the mid-twenties that a new straight stretch was constructed and called Amersham Road. Mrs. Nancy Thomas tells of her husband cycling along the newly-built road in about 1926. By 1930, building plots were being offered for sale, and houses were erected by Captain Freeborn on land bought from Darvells of Chorleywood. A sketch map shows a proposed road opposite the end of Church Grove on the Chenies side of the Sheep-houses, but in the event this was never constructed.

A further opening up of the district took place on June 27th 1935, when the Duke of Bedford offered 106 acres of building land for sale at auction.[27] The sale brochure was addressed to 'Speculators, Builders and Others', and described the land as being 'Ripe for immediate development'. The first three lots, amounting to some 30 acres and called 'Church Grove Estate', covered the ground between the railway line and the main road. They were sold together for £250 per acre, and became Oakington Avenue and Amersham Way. The ancient copse of trees from which Church Grove derives its name was then still standing (between Church Grove and Oakington Avenue). The remaining lots were for land at Chorleywood. According to Kelly's Directory of Amersham and Chesham, there were approximately 300 houses in Little Chalfont in 1939; thus the population would have reached about one thousand, a five-fold increase since the end of the first world war.

In November 1936, the Bucks Examiner[29] thought it would have a little fun at our expense:

> **LITTLE CHALFONT AND THE WASHING**
> Last week there appeared in the daily press, a report of an action concerning the hanging out of washing, one of the particular offences alleged against a family in a residential estate, being that they hung out washing on a Sunday. The County Judge held that:
>
> > No washing must be displayed on Sundays.
>
> A resident, living in the Little Chalfont area, forwards us the cutting, and asks us to quote. Well, we have obliged the lady. This is her reason:
>
> > Perhaps some such time limit would be helpful locally, for it is quite a common sight to see washing displayed here every Sunday, and by many one would expect to be "far too superior to do washing at all".

That is an unkind cut - what have the ladies (presumably the alleged offenders are not gentlemen) who offend got to say about it? Is Little Chalfont so superior that folk do not wash - referring to clothes of course, and not bodies.

Bottle Cottage in Finch Lane.

Bell Lane in the early 1920s taken from the main road.

Thatched houses in Chalfont Station Village in the mid-1920s.

Aerial view of village taken in 1933 by Mr Wright, an amateur pilot.

Junction of Church Grove and Amersham Road. The straight section of the main road was only constructed in the mid-1920s.

Village centre with the "Donkey Field" on the left.

Berkeley and Son, Family Butchers at Nightingales Corner.

Norman Lofts Ironmongers shop, one of the first to open at Nightingales Corner in 1930.

Local Firms and Telephones

Bearing in mind the predominantly rural scene at the turn of the century, it is hardly surprising that the first businesses to start up were agricultural ones. Clark of Amersham Common provided steam engines for road works and farm threshing, as did Grovers in the White Lion Road opposite Beel House Lodge. The first major firm, however, was Boughtons, which was founded in 1897 by Thomas Trafford (TT) Boughton, whose family had been involved in running water mills and farms near the River Chess for about two hundred years. As he grew up, Thomas became much more interested in engines than in farming, and at the age of about twenty-five bought land at Bell Lane from Lord Chesham. To help him start in business, his father, John, offered to buy a new steam engine. The year 1897 was Queen Victoria's Diamond Jubilee, and the Royal Counties Show at Reading had on display all the latest machines. Over seventy shining monsters were on view, and after much deliberation, John and Thomas chose one named 'Black Jack'. It gave wonderful service for over fifty years, and is still owned by the company. It is often seen being driven to steam fairgrounds, and even took part in the London Lord Mayor's Show in 1978!

For most of the early years, Boughtons operated as contractors undertaking steam ploughing and threshing, and also timber cutting and haulage. The family house built on the site was immediately adjacent to the works, which were always known as 'The Yard', and when the day's work had ended, the telephone used to be switched through to the house, thus providing a twenty-four hour service. According to TT's son John,[30] there was no electricity, gas, water or drainage laid on, and they had to generate their own power supply from a paraffin-fuelled engine, backed up by open-top lead-acid batteries. Because there was no mains water, rain was collected from the roofs and stored in large tanks. Steam engines naturally needed considerable quantities, and in summertime they used to drive down to the Chess, or to the pond at Finch Lane, to top-up supplies. TT often used to say of those days:

> It was not difficult to get a pint of beer, a wedge of bread and cheese, a pickled onion and a punch on the head, all for the princely sum of 2d.

Over the next twenty years, many new and second-hand steam engines were purchased, until more than twenty were operating. During the years of the depression, competition was severe and they had to search far afield for any sort of work available. Much of this came from the programme of road improvements necessitated by the growth of cars and lorries, and from the development of housing estates. One of the most unusual contracts was for the transportation of circus animals to Whipsnade at the beginning of 1931, around the time it was being opened.

Early in 1941, Boughtons were informed by the War Office that the entire beech woods from Chenies towards Chesham had to be cut down to provide rifle butts for the army, and that they had been allocated the job. After much searching around for extra engines, they were able to cut and deliver to the saw mills in High Wycombe the quota of one thousand cubic feet per day. The family were distressed at their part in destroying these beloved beechwoods, but the demands of war had to come first. There was a rumour that, in the event, the timber was not needed for rifle butts.

With the gradual demise of steam, the firm developed its saw mill on the Bell Lane site, but eventually sold out to a High Wycombe furniture company. Boughtons then decided to concentrate on manufacturing equipment and machinery for specialist applications, and have opened other factories in Devon. It is still a family-run concern, with first the sons and then the grandsons of Thomas carrying on the business.

Another business which is very much part of the village scene, is Munn & Chapmans Garage and Showrooms. In the early 1920s, Mr. Chapman, who lived at the end of Amersham Common, operated a horse-drawn carriage service at Chalfont and Latimer Station. He worked from old wooden sheds below the bank in the space now taken by the lower car park by Bedford Avenue, and these sheds can just be discerned in old photographs. While he waited for customers to arrive at the station, the horses were turned loose in a nearby field. A telephone was installed for people to ring when they required him to pick them up.

The story can now be picked up from a letter written by Mr. Len Munn from Guernsey in September 1983:

> In 1922 my parents moved into the village of Chenies, my father being chauffeur at Woodside House, and among other duties, had to drive his employer to either Chalfont and Latimer or alternatively Chorleywood station. During the next few years, my father realised the possibility of a motor taxi service from Chalfont station, since the only transport then available was a horse-drawn taxi, which was operated by Mr. Chapman.
>
> Since the cab route was issued by licence from the Metropolitan Railway, it was obvious that he would have to involve Mr. Chapman. At that time, 1926, there was only one entrance to the station (on the UP line) and the horses and cab were kept in wooden sheds. Mr. Chapman was then used to answer the telephone, and my father had the task of driving the motor taxi. This was followed by the installation of a petrol pump at the bottom of the hill to the station, and the employment of a motor mechanic to repair the limited number of vehicles in the area. He progressed at some pace. Due

Boughton's Yard at the turn of the century.

Munn & Chapman's Garage in the 1930s.

to pressure of work, he employed another driver and purchased another vehicle (Daimler). He also purchased a Chevrolet lorry, got a driver, and used to cart coal from the waggons in the goods yard, to the big houses in the Chalfont St. Giles area. These included Bertram Mills (of circus fame) and the Maharaja of Patiola who lived at the Vache.

At the beginning of 1928, my father bought two 21 foot plots of land from Mr. Darvil of Chesham, and built the main part of our present premises with living accommodation over the garage. We naturally moved in and lived over the shop so to speak.

In 1932, two brothers named Clifton bought a vacant plot next door to our garage, on the station side, and built a shop and flat to the same frontal design as our garage. They opened a radio and electrical business named Clifton Bros. However, they had to close down, and in 1934 my father bought the building and turned it into a small showroom with offices behind. About the same time, my father bought another 21 foot plot next to our garage, and sold the front half to Mr. Kipling who lived in Village Way. In the back half, we built a further workshop to link up with the original building. Mr. Kipling then built a shop and flat above, again to our original design. It was for Mr. Kipling's son Kenneth, who set up a shop selling greengroceries, flowers and fruit.

I cannot recall the exact date, but certainly about 1933, the plot next to Kiplings' was purchased by E. S. Gates and used for his office. This I bought in 1964, and Kiplings' half plot was finally bought back in 1976, thus enabling my sons to develop the site which you see today.

Statter Switchgear was a large and world-renowned engineering company, with offices on the site now occupied by Amersham International plc and by Halifax House. In 1920 John Grice Statter and Major (later Lt-Colonel) Marston, who was still serving in the War Office, started the company. A wooden shed behind the shops at Nightingales Corner was built by Major Marston during weekend leaves, as their first works for manufacturing industrial switchgear. For accommodation during these weekends, he erected a bell tent close by. Initially boys were mainly employed, but, with no machine tools, parts had to be made in Chesham and collected by bicycle. Major Marston DSO MC brought the verve, enthusiasm and engineering experience, whilst John Statter, who operated from the corner of a small office in Victoria Street shared with other companies, brought the sales and business experience. In the early days, goods were dispatched to the station by horse drawn vans for onwards transport.

By 1925, larger works were needed, but they were only able to acquire the present Amersham International site, which then comprised unwanted land formed by the railway embankments and the main road, with practically no level ground. Initially, buildings consisted of one bay of the machine shop, with lathes driven by a diesel engine via overhead shafts and leather belts, and a small brick erection, in which Col. Marston had an office, on the outside of which were stairs made from an old London double-decker bus, complete with advertisements. Later on, he took over the house at the front of the site called 'Ten Turrets'.

During the slump in the late twenties and early thirties, times were difficult and wages could not be increased. Few new employees could be taken on, but the switchgear produced was of the highest quality, and was exported throughout the world. Engineers were sent overseas to many countries, in order to negotiate contracts and to commission equipment. By the mid-thirties, with the recession over and the development of industry and housing restarting, the business prospered. The works were extended and a foundry built. From 1938 onwards, Admiralty orders for warships increased enormously, as did the work for war-time factories.

At the end of the war, a separate factory was acquired in Raans Road, to provide plastic mouldings for the switchgear, as outside suppliers had been found unreliable. At first there was insufficient work for the presses, so contracts were obtained from Woolworths and others, for plastic roundabouts, toy boats, ash trays and Christmas tree lighting sets. During this period, a fitting shop was built in the White Lion Road, and a foundry was acquired in Chesham. At its peak, the company employed more than seven hundred people.

By the mid-1950s, competition became fiercer, and many companies had to combine. In November 1956, Statters became part of Lancashire Dynamo Group, with Col. Marston as Chairman of the whole group. Four years later, however, a takeover battle was won by Metal Industries, who promptly sold Statters to English Electric, which subsequently became part of GEC. The factory finally closed in 1972.

People who worked for the firm and were proud of it say that nothing was the same again. Col. Marston had been the driving force behind the company, and was very much respected by his staff. People recall the sports and tea parties which he held in the grounds of Garden Reach, his house in Burtons Lane. He died in 1961, and an obituary notice recorded that there were many individuals who would remember help, often of a most generous character, received from him in an hour of need, on condition that his benevolence should not be disclosed.

Advertisement in The Electrical Times dated May 1938, emphasising the firm's international status.

Another business which was established in the village was known as Station Garages. The buildings next to the station by the railway bridge were originally Graham's Garage in the early 1930s, and the name can clearly be seen on an old London Transport photograph. They were then taken over in 1933 by Mr. Wright, who with his wife Doreen built up a flourishing motor car repair and sales organisation. Part of the site was, for a time, occupied by an electrical firm named Gilberts. The lower section of the building was also used as a car showroom, but was found to be in a poor position to attract customers. Later on, the Wrights put up a much larger showroom in the station approach, and this is now the Tyre and Exhaust centre.

Nowadays, the largest business concern in Little Chalfont is undoubtedly Amersham International plc, with sites on the White Lion Road, at Pollards Wood in Nightingales Lane, and in the centre of the village. It has markets worldwide, in the fields of medical diagnostics, research products and radiation sources. The beginnings, however, were on a much smaller scale. In 1940, a small company, Thorium Limited, was invited by the Government to undertake the refining of radium and the manufacture of radium-based luminous paint for use on compasses, gunsights and aircraft instruments. Chilcote House near to the White Lion public house was purchased, and work started in May 1940. Within a few years, the work was broadened to include some of the products derived from the nuclear reactor programme, and the Radiochemical Centre was formed. During the 1950s, the emphasis changed from radium-based products towards pharmaceuticals and research chemicals. In 1954, the Centre became part of the new United Kingdom Atomic Energy Authority.

Expansion continued throughout the 1960s, and many new offices and laboratories were built on the White Lion site; the first cyclotron was also installed, and over 600 staff were employed. In 1971, the Centre became a private limited company, in recognition of its success and of the need for greater commercial freedom. By then, the original site was running out of space for expansion, and a major site was started at Cardiff, which in time doubled the manufacturing capacity, leading to the employment worldwide of more than 2000 staff. In the early 1980s, the company was selected by the Government as one of the first for privatisation, and shortly afterwards the name was changed to the present one of Amersham International.

TELEPHONES

Most people have a telephone these days, or at least ready access to one, and we take it for granted that we can dial almost anywhere in the world. But in 1907, there were only twenty exchanges in the whole of Buckinghamshire, one of which was at Amersham (it had been opened in 1902). In September 1907, the Post Office Gazette[31] announced that:

A Sub-Exchange and Call office will be opened at Amersham Common on the 25th. The hours of attendance will be Weekdays from 7am to 8pm, and Sundays from 7am to 7.15am, and 8am to 10am.

It would be interesting to find out why the telephone operator did not have to attend the switchboard for the intervening forty-five minutes! By 1923, there were only forty-five customers at Amersham Common, and only just over a hundred at Amersham itself. One of the earliest users was Boughtons in Bell Lane, who were proud of their number: Amersham Common 5. Mrs. Sylvia Flitney remembers that her father Percy West rented the 'Old Amersham Common' Post Office immediately after the end of the First World War from Mr. Forwood of Bendrose Farm. This old building is now the betting shop near the Pineapple public house. The Post Office part was moved to the present premises opposite Flack's Garage in 1932. In 1930, it was announced that

The name of the present Amersham Common Exchange, in the Reading District, will be changed to 'Little Chalfont', as from the 1st April.

Not only was the name changed, but the two operator switchboards were moved into Mr. Rhodes' Oxford Store, into a room at the back which is now the space behind the Post Office counter. Shortly after this transfer, there were just over two hundred subscribers, served by two full-time operators. One was Mrs. Anne Hearn who now lives in Amersham, and who remembers having to cycle to work from Chesham Bois. She was not afraid, even in the dark late at night, except once when she completely lost her way in a thick fog. The second operator, Elsie Lambert, now lives in Chesham. A little later on, Doris Wheeler took over from Mrs. Hearn.

It seems there were powerful local voices demanding the latest automatic system, because a new building was put up in 1935, as shown by a plaque on the wall. In those days, very few rural exchanges had been converted to automatic working, and Amersham itself did not change until 1960. The Bucks Examiner published the following article on its front page on 30th October 1937:

LITTLE CHALFONT - FROM MANUAL TO AUTOMATIC
For some time now there has been work going on at Little Chalfont, which has revolutionised the telephone system in that area. No-one outside has realised the important and intricate nature of the work, but to the P.O. Engineering Department, it has been a work of art, culminating on Saturday 24th October, with the transfer

of the local telephone system from manual to automatic. What might be termed the critical time was about 1.30 on Saturday afternoon, when a number of officials and operators were grouped round the old switchboard watching the in-coming and out-going calls. At a specified time, all the 'traffic' was cleared, and special arrangements were made to deal with emergency calls. For the few minutes when subscribers could neither give nor receive calls, the engineers worked methodically to effect the great change, and the work was carried through without a hitch and without delay. The operators, who will not be displaced, but transferred to other local exchanges, put away their headphones, and started testing the subscribers' instruments, and giving them the necessary instructions.

To attempt to describe the new exchange is far too technical for the layman, suffice to say that subscribers who are interested, can always see the works 'on request'. To see the intricacies of the exchange is to see some amazing engineering, and a visit is worthwhile.

Finally, the exchange was converted to 'digital electronic' in 1990, and there are now about four thousand subscribers. It is strange that the word 'subscriber', which was coined over a hundred years ago, is still used to describe telephone 'customers'.

One of Broughton's pre-War steam lorries.

Steam engine owned by William Clark of Amersham Common.

Statter's office known as "Ten Turrets" shortly before being demolished in the early 1980s.

One of Statter's workshops where Amersham International headquarters now stands.

Post-War group of workers at Statter's Switchgear.
At one stage the firm employed over 700 people.

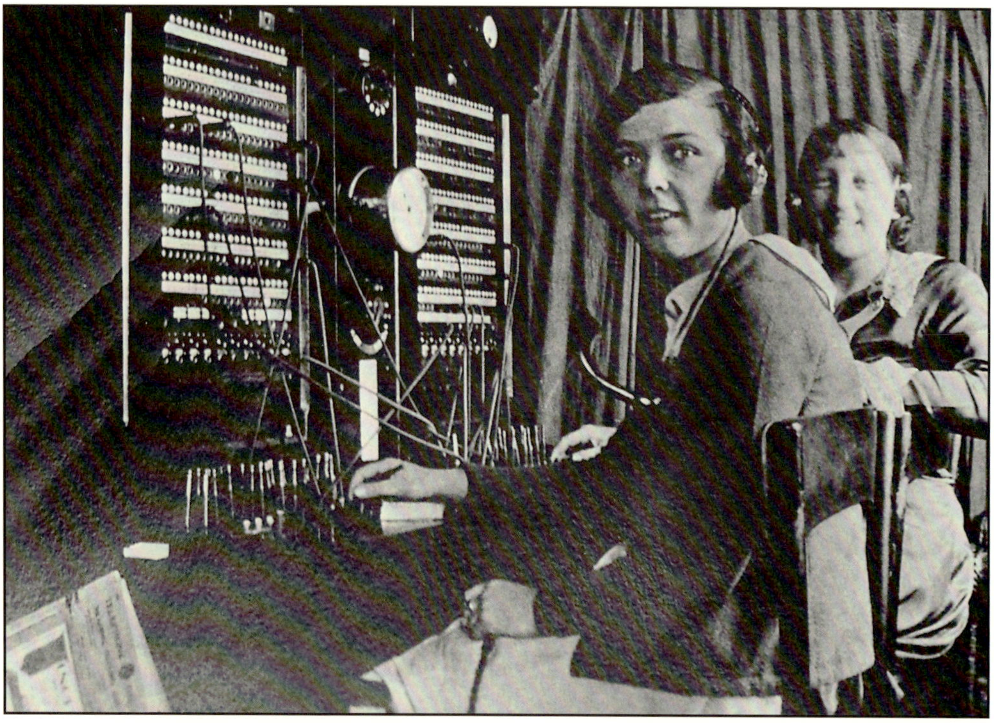

Anne Hearn and Elsie Lambert at the telephone swichboard housed at the Oxford Store, taken in 1930.

War Time

The following notice appeared in the Bucks Examiner in 1941, by which time the war had lasted for two years. Naturally the censors permitted very little of national importance to be reported in local papers, and the stories which follow have been related by people living here at the time.

> LITTLE CHALFONT - BEWARE
>
> Police and Civil Defence Services will participate in a Home Guard exercise which will take place in the Little Chalfont and Chenies area on Sunday, Sept. 14th, between 9am and noon.
>
> War conditions will be simulated. Residents and others passing through or about the area, may expect to be asked to show their Registration Cards, and those without Gas Masks, may be delayed or diverted by other routes.

Several residents have recalled strings of elephants ambling through the village centre on their way from the station to Pollards Wood in Nightingales Lane, each holding the tail in front with its trunk. This house was the home for many years of the celebrated circus proprietor, Bertram Mills and his family, but of course, animals were not normally kept there.

Bertram Mills was a Freeman of the City of London Loriners and Farriers Companies, and prior to 1914 was in the carriage-building and harness-manufacturing business. He was also a breeder and international judge of Hackney harness horses, and this was his preoccupation until 1920 when, at the age of forty-seven, he founded the Bertram Mills Circus, produced annually at Olympia. It was not until 1929 that he branched out again by organising a travelling tented circus, making it possible to stage performances in numerous cities throughout the country. He died in 1938, aged sixty-five, but his wife Ethel stayed on at Pollards Wood, leaving their two sons to carry on the business.

In the book 'Bertram Mills Circus', written by his son Cyril, the problems of trying to adjust to wartime conditions are described thus:

> That Sunday was September 3rd 1939, and we heard we were at war. It looked as though the circus had had it, and nobody was sure we would not be bombed that night. Everything was torn down, and we began the trek back to Ascot. Tents and equipment were packed into the sheds where they would remain for the duration; animals went to their stables and dens, but what would happen to them was unknown. On the fourth day, when our work was nearly finished, a man in uniform walked

in and told us that the place had been requisitioned, and that we must get out at once. It was to become an internment camp.

Fortunately, Mother was still living at Pollards Wood, where there were loose boxes for thirty-five or forty horses. There had been a sale after Father's death and about twenty of his coaches, and all his hunters, jumpers and hackneys had been sold; so by making each loose box into two stalls, and a coach house into an elephant shed, we were able to house all the domestic animals. One of the two large riding schools housed the wild animals, and the other provided an exercise ring for the horses, ponies and elephants, and space for a dozen of the more valuable caravans. The rest of the caravans and trailers had to be scattered in the woods, so that they could not be seen from the air or from the road in what was essentially a residential area.

Various people remember the wild animals roaring, from even as far away as the village centre. Mrs. Joan Adamson, living near Cokes Farm, relates how puzzled she was when her cat used to come home in the evenings carrying a lump of raw meat. It was not until some time later that she realised the cat must have been going into the lions' cages, and stealing the food. She also states that Bertram Mills had a practice ring in the grounds, and that Tom Tagg was the ring-master.

Mrs. Adamson recalls that a group of volunteer civilians used to drive a mobile canteen round the village, providing meals to various service units. Wartime meals were also served at the Golden Hind tea rooms opposite Nightingales Corner, and Statters Recreation Club also used the premises. Others remember long queues forming outside the tea rooms when cakes were sometimes available on Saturday mornings.

A factory making clothing for the war effort was housed in wooden sheds in Loudhams Road close to the Statters works. Named Williams Clothing, it eventually expanded into three sheds, which were later acquired by Statters. The Station Garage had to close for the duration of the war, presumably due to lack of petrol or cars to sell, and the premises were used to store unused ice-cream vans. Somewhat ironically, however, a strategic petrol store of one million gallons' capacity was located in Bedford Avenue on the site of the lower car park. Church Grove also had a role to play, in that a temporary fire station was placed there, consisting of a small truck and a red bucket.

Mr. Ray Edmunds, who worked all his life at Statters, was very much involved in keeping up the morale of workers and local residents by helping to organise ENSA concerts and parties. These were laid on either in the works canteen, or in the Home Guard hut nearby. One of the performances offered the following programme, including free refreshments:

STATTER'S FOLLIES 1943
PROGRAMME

1. *Company*
2. *Megan Scott*
3. *'The Artistic Touch' with Ivy Allsopp & Joe Esterton*
4. *Ted Rutherford - Comedian*
5. *Eastern Magic*
6. *Frank Howe - Ukulele*
7. *Trick Cyclist - Pete Barlow & John East*
8. *Megan Scott - Soprano*
9. *Pamela Kerr-Bock - Monologue*
10. *Ted Dwight - Tenor*
11. *Company*

INTERVAL - REFRESHMENTS WITH MUSICAL ACCOMMPANIMENT

12. *Company*
13. *Shakespeare*
14. *'The Village Pub' with Ivy Allsopp, Peggy Simmonds, Winnie King, Ted Ennew, Sid Aris & Ted Rutherford*
15. *Ray Edmunds - Accordion*
16. *'Napoleon' - Steel & Co.*
17. *Kath Orchard & Ray Edmunds in Harmony*
18. *Megan Scott*
19. *'Tug-o-War - Steel & Co.*
20. *'The Advice Bureau' with Megan Scott, Winnie King, Sid Aris, Frank Howe, Joe Esterton, Marco & Pete Barlow*
21. *Cliff Lacey*
22. *Kath Orchard - Crooner*
23. *Finale - Ted Dwight, Ted Rutherford, John East & Company*

Musical Accompaniment - Ray Edmunds
Rhythmical - Cliff Lacey
Stage Manager - T. Chaney
Stage Electrician - C. Nix
Produced by - F. Howe

Home Guard platoon photographed near the station. Mr Bowler, the chimney sweep is second on the left in the middle row.

Knife sharpening in Amersham Way.

Little Chalfont may have been relatively unscathed by the war, being perhaps just too far from London to be affected by air raids there, but Mrs. Nancy Thomas wrote about two aircraft accidents which, by an amazing coincidence, occurred within a week of each other. She is writing from her home in Church Grove:

NOT SO QUIET DOWN HERE

Under this title I originally set down the story of our household's involvement in two wartime incidents of March 1944. The account was written down a few days after the incident of 30th March as part of a letter to a correspondence circle of friends, at that time widely scattered up and down the country. The following account of that incident is extracted from my letter:

One sometimes hears of competitions where people have to describe the worst moment of their lives. Well, I think my worst one up to date was this month. I woke one night about ten past twelve to hear the rattle of machine guns somewhere overhead and realised there was a raid on. The sound of the dog-fight died away, and I lay listening to distant intermittent gunfire, which eventually got closer, so I slid quietly out and pulled my things on. I hoped Jack would not wake for he had gone to bed early, filled up with hot milk and brandy in an attempt to kill a filthy cold. However, he did wake and got his things on, but I persuaded him to lie under the eiderdown and keep warm, while I went to Rosemary who had awakened by now. It seemed a distant and not very bad raid, and I hoped Pat would not wake. I sat on R's bed and amused myself reading one of her books while she tried to sleep again.

Things quieted down and I was expecting the All Clear would soon sound, when the guns started up again. I groaned inwardly and hoped this would be the last wave, and then I heard an aircraft, coming our way, and I realised too late it was diving. The roar grew to a deafening pitch and I instinctively ducked as I put a steadying hand on Rosemary, and said to myself in the words of the RAF, "This is it". But the roar passed overhead, lessened a little and then stopped dead. I straightened again, thought "No, it isn't", and dived for the stairs to see at the front door whether it was in the field outside, shouting for Jack at the same time and wondering whether the plane still had its bomb load on board. Eric beat me to it to the door, and there we could see she was on the far side of the wood, blazing furiously and with ammunition popping off in all directions. We evidently were not likely to be flattened if anything heavy went off. By this time Betty was awake - she had not heard a thing - and Eric sent her to the phone to notify the Home Guard C.O., while he got into his uniform. I dashed upstairs to quieten the excited children, drag Jack's Sten (gun) off its hook and get his ammunition out while he tumbled into uniform, and incidentally to drop a few words of caution lest he fall in with a truculent Jerry airman.

The fire engines rolled past and soon the C.O. appeared and the nearest Home Guard platoon was mustered and they were all set to go out and collect Nazis. 'The Croft' became temporary Home Guard Headquarters and we were told to take any phone messages and pass them out to the C.O. We promptly set to work to brew tea for anyone who needed it. Meanwhile the All Clear had sounded, more or less unnoticed, and the children all camped in a row on the girls' window seat to watch the fire engines filling up from the nearest hydrant outside our gate. A stray Home Guard came in for a cup of tea, and, hearing a strange voice, the children immediately concluded a Jerry had been brought in and came scrambling down to have a look-see. How their faces fell when they found it was Sergeant L. instead of a Jerry! By now, alas, the news had come through that it was not a Jerry, but one of our bombers on its way back from Germany, partly disabled and off its course, so the Home Guard, all elation flattened, set out to look for the rest of the crew, some of whom were still unaccounted for. The pilot, poor fellow, had broken his neck in the crash, but the rest of the crew were all eventually found all right. How the two who also came down with the wreck escaped with nothing but shock is a mystery to us all, for the plane was blazing and fell to pieces over about four fields. It was a Canadian crew and one of them remarked "I'm a man who rides on the edge of eternity!"

The excitement gradually died away and we packed the children off to bed again with a drink of glucose and milk, and Betty and I sat by the phone waiting for the men to come in. It was 3.15am when the Home Guard were eventually stood down and we got back to bed. A reliable man who had seen the whole incident told us afterwards that the plane was about 300 ft. up when she went over this house, and he felt certain we were doomed as he saw it coming, but had no time to warn us. I don't think I like sudden death passing within 100 yards. It's an unsettling feeling. All the weekend, of course, this bit of countryside was beset with sightseers, some of them from miles away. Had it been a Jerry, it would have been understandable, but I cannot follow the morbid curiosity that brings people miles to look at the pitiful heap of wreckage that had been one of our own planes.

It was about a week later that I could not get to sleep one night. There were a lot of very low-flying aircraft about, and I was grousing to Jack that I wished I had not heard the noise of the falling plane the week before, as now low planes at night seemed to make me uneasy. He very sensibly pointed out that the chance of one hitting us was about one in ten thousand, particularly after having had one so close. I agreed that he was probably right and eventually dropped off to sleep during a lull in the noise. I slept solidly through until his alarm clock happened to wake me at 5.45am, and I was vaguely aware of him partly dressed and going down to put his breakfast kettle on. There were more aircraft about, including one very low, but I never take much notice of them at that time of the morning and just on daylight too. Suddenly I realised Betty was shouting insistently to Jack, who was apparently outside getting some coal. The girls woke up and wanted to know what the matter was. Bother me if there wasn't another bomber down in a field, at the back this time. "Is it burning?" I yelled. "No", said Betty, and I rolled over feeling dopily that it did not concern me then. Jack came into the bedroom and grabbed a jacket and said he was going over to see if there was any help needed. Betty fell into some clothes and went after him with a brandy flask, and then I suddenly came to, realising that there might be injured men, and that at any rate, there were probably weary and thirsty men who would want hot tea and a phone.

I got out and into dressing gown and slippers. I ran out onto the green in front of the gate. Yes, there she was sitting quietly in the middle of a ploughed field and there were some of the crew coming away from her with Jack. I went back and put on a large kettle and put the grill going for toast. Eric was once again phoning the Home Guard C.O, and within a quarter of an hour of that crash, three members of the crew were sitting round the dining-room fire drinking tea and eating toast and crab apple jelly. (One felt so troubled at not having more lavish fare to offer, but the strict rationing of those days gave little chance of building up a reserve for unexpected needs.) Two of the others were in another house at the back of us, and later the last man came over to us and also had some breakfast.

It was a mixed crew of four British and two Canadians under a Yankee pilot. The children, of course, were thrilled to the marrow. They had dressed themselves at a perfectly incredible speed and now sat in a bunch goggling at their first real live bomber crew. Meanwhile a Home Guard picket was around the plane and soon the local police constable turned up to take a statement—and a cup of tea—and after much telephoning we once more settled down to something like normal again and got the children safely off to school on time; I don't know how (for their protests were loud for fear of missing something). Rosemary got the autographs of all our four and was duly puffed up about it, especially as the American pilot added a flowery little 'sentiment' to his signature.

The crew could not speak highly enough of the pilot. They thought he was simply 'wizard' and he certainly pulled off a wizard landing. Apparently they were down to their last two gallons of petrol after a tough trip somewhere, Nuremberg we presume, though they did not say and we did not ask. He had touched down first at the far end of a long pasture field and had not seen a rather sunken lane edged with trees, owing to ground mist, until he was on top of it. However, he managed to get over the lane through the biggest gap in the trees, only losing about fifteen feet of one wing getting through. One landing wheel had gone neatly through a gateway and the other had ripped through the hedge. Then, seeing he was making straight for an iron fence and the road, he had turned her up towards the middle of the field and come to rest beside a fold of ewes and lambs. An all-round ticklish job I should imagine landing at 140 miles an hour under those conditions. The British members of the crew said this was their third crash, and all on Fridays!

The plane is being dismantled and taken away now, and of course there is a crash guard on it from the nearest RAF station, so we frequently have various members of the guard in here of an evening for a sit by the fire and a snack. The set that were here on Good Friday were a lively gang, and told us some interesting yarns, but they kept us up until well after midnight talking, bless their hearts. Well, we've had one in the front and one at the back; I only hope the third isn't in the middle!

Corner of Westwood Park looking towards the Village of Chenies.

Oxford Stores and Post Office in the late 1930s, with Dudley Rhode's brother.

The village centre in 1938. Teas were served at the "Sugar Loaves".

The Sugar Loaves and Rendezvous from Village Way. The trees are now quite mature.

View of Burtons Lane dating from the 1950s.

The Old and New Village Halls

On June 16th 1950, the 1st Chenies and Chalfont Brownie Pack recorded in their Log Book:

> Mr. Myerscough came and took photos of the Pack, especially to get a good one of a 'Brownie Smile'. This night Chalfont Hall was burnt down but we were not the last people to use it!

Many residents will not be aware that there have been two village halls on different sites. The Old Hall, otherwise known as the Home Guard Hut, was donated by Col. Marston of Statters at the beginning of the last war, and was erected on a vacant plot between Munn and Chapman's garage and the Bank next to the Sugar Loaves. It was mainly used by local platoons of the Home Guard for meetings and training, but it was also available to clubs, groups, Scouts, Guides and to Statters for their wartime concerts. The Afternoon Women's Institute, founded in 1946, regularly held its meetings there, and also ran a weekly produce stall on the pavement outside. The stall continued to be a feature of village life until the mid-1960s. In 1950, the WI decided to donate an electric clock for use inside the hall, and it was duly fitted. It has been stated that it was on the very day that the clock was connected that the fire occurred. Being wooden, the building would have burned quickly, giving the fire brigade no chance. Mr. Len Munn recalled that the side wall of his garage was damaged.

The hall had been insured for £1100, and this formed the nucleus of a new hall fund. The WI were enthusiastic in raising money, and had plans for a £5000 building, but in the end they had to be content with a smaller one. The local council made a grant of £1000, and other funds came from a WI pie scheme £300, waste paper £134, fete £100, jumble sale £45, piano fund £32, appeal letter £257, and the Scouts and Guides £5 each. Altogether £936 was raised! The new hall cost £2890, the difference being bridged by a council loan which was repaid in less than ten years. The building was erected on the present site, on land donated by the District Council.

The opening ceremony took place on Saturday 8th November 1952[32] with Councillor Major Boyce in the Chair, and the Revd. A G Kesseck of St, George's Church conducting the dedication service. Mr. Leslie Myerscough then sang 'Bless this House'. At the instance of Col. Marston, three cheers were given for the Managing Committee for all they had done. Col. Marston paid particular tribute to the ladies for their untiring help. The function concluded with the National Anthem.

Mrs. Doreen Wright, who was a founder member of the Afternoon WI and helped to design their banner, which is still in use, remembers that a local trader, Mr. Dunfee, had bought a very large consignment of surplus naval ammunition boxes made of excellent teak. The original floor of the new hall was constructed from these boxes.

During the next twenty-five years, the hall was run by the 'Village Hall Committee', consisting mainly of volunteers from various local groups such as the WI, plus nominated council representatives. Virtually all repair jobs were carried out by the wives and husbands of these members, with Mr. Don Fulkes, especially, spending a great deal of his time at the hall most days. One weekend, a dozen or more enthusiasts stripped the surface of the wood floor, and then repolished it. Mr. John Powell, now Councillor Powell, with the blessing of Statters, used to arrange repairs to broken equipment and look after any electrical problems. He served on the committee for many years, and was Chairman for about fifteen of them.

During this period, the hall roof was inhabited by a large family of edible dormice known as Glisglis. Lord Rothschild introduced this variety of dormouse into the country in 1902, thinking it would be nice to add them to his collection of birds and animals at his estate at Tring. Some time later, a number of them escaped from captivity, and started to colonise the surrounding countryside; one group settling in Little Chalfont.

By the 1970s, however, difficulties arose on the financial side, and the District Council found itself being asked regularly to contribute funds. In the end, an arrangement was made whereby the District Council assumed responsibility for the hall as from April 1978, but leased it immediately to Amersham Town Council at a nominal rent. Recalling that 'Bless This House' had been sung at the dedication service, the WI Evening Institute sent a greetings card and good wishes to the Town Council saying:

Bless this house O' Lord we pray
Keep it filled by night and day;
Keep it warm that we may find
Teeth don't chatter and draughts unkind
Freeze us blue within the hour
In spite of friendship's warming pow'r!
We've sat through meetings within these walls
In absolute misery warmed by anger alone!

Unable to reach, by letter or 'phone
Anyone to answer our plea;
Please come along if only to see
Just how cold this hall can be.
We wish the Town Council well
And hope this will prove the end of our troubles,
The beginning of days when this hall
Is blessed with true warmth and praise!

In 1989, the council carried out a major refurbishment, building new outside walls, a new kitchen, and a toilet at the rear for handicapped people. A new heating system was installed, and the floor was replaced. At the same time, the old permanent stage was removed and replaced by movable sections which can be adapted for various purposes. The hall continues to be fully booked, serving both local users and commercial enterprises, and these lettings suffice to cover all costs.

At the rear of the hall are a number of smaller wooden sheds, which are used to store equipment for some of the users, such as the Guides and Brownies, and also the Chiltern Players. This amateur dramatic group was founded by Linden Barnett in 1953 and, with only an occasional break, has presented two shows a year ever since. It has consistently achieved first-class performances, in terms both of acting and of stage production, and has attracted its own set of enthusiastic followers. In the early days, with very little live theatre available, the hall foyer was absolutely packed for performances, and queues used to stretch into Cokes Lane. In those days, seating for 160 people was allowed. Under new safety regulations, however, the capacity has been reduced to 84, and this has made it much more difficult to cover costs from ticket sales. The lack of a permanent stage has also introduced new challenges for the set designers.

Stony Lane looking towards the main road.

LITTLE CHALFONT HALL

THE OPENING CEREMONY
AND DEDICATION OF THE
NEW HALL IN COKES LANE

will be held on

Saturday, 8th November, 1952

at 3 p.m.

Chairman : MAJOR G. BOYCE, M.B.E., M.C.

All members of the community are invited to attend

MASON, Printer, Amersham

Opening ceremony of the new Village Hall.

The Village Hall, 1993.

Developments since the End of the War

As has been seen, a considerable amount of building work took place from the mid-1920s up to the outbreak of war. By then, most of the houses along the White Lion Road had been constructed, as well as those in Village Way, along Burtons and Cokes Lanes, Amersham Way, and parts of Church Grove and Amersham Road. However, north of the railway line, looking towards Latimer and the Chess valley, virtually nothing had been built, with probably less than a dozen houses altogether in Chenies and Beechwood Avenues. Because of shortages of materials, new houses were effectively rationed, and building permits were required. Even when they were granted, no more than a thousand square feet of accommodation was allowed. These restrictions remained in force until about 1955, with the result that very few new houses were erected. When at last they were relaxed, development restarted in earnest, and over the following twenty years most of the post-war programme was carried out.

An aerial photograph of the village, taken in the 1930s, shows many tracks across fields where people had taken the direct route from home to the station. From Beechwood and Chenies Avenues, it was possible, even until the late 1950s, to walk across two fields to the foot of the railway bank in Bedford Avenue. These fields are now, of course, occupied by the houses in Westwood Drive, Elizabeth Avenue and Russell Close. There were no steps up to the station from Bedford Avenue, but people used to scramble up the bank via a steep and muddy track. Other short cuts which show up well on the photograph run from the Sheephouses to the station, and from Burtons Lane across the 'Donkey Field' (behind the present shopping parade) to emerge opposite the Post Office.

The council houses on the estate at the Bell Lane end of Elizabeth Avenue were among the first to be built in the early 1950s. The Avenue, however, did not then run all the way from Bell Lane through to the main road; the section between Chenies Avenue and the new estate was, at that time, only an old farm track. Until 1953, the part from Chenies Avenue to the main road was called Latimer Avenue, and it was to celebrate the coronation of the Queen that the name was changed to Elizabeth Avenue. Grad Builders started the bungalows there the following year, but the road was not surfaced until about 1962. Until then, there were deep potholes, no footpaths, and some remnants of the old hedge. After heavy rain storms, a lake formed from verge to verge some two hundred yards long, on which children used to play with their toy boats.

Bedford Avenue and lower Chenies Avenue were the next to be built, also by Grad. Oldfield Close was built to provide housing for the growing numbers of Radiochemical workers; finally, Oakington Avenue was extended through to the main road to form the road as we now know it, and the bungalows were built.

In an attempt to balance the growing pressures to provide land for residential development on the one hand, and the need to preserve the Green

Belt on the other, the County Council published a Little Chalfont Town Map[2] in 1964, accompanied by a written statement. The intention was to designate areas for residential, industrial and commercial use. The map covered an area of about 2300 acres, and present-day readers will decide for themselves to what extent the following aim of the plan has been realised:

> It will be the policy of the County Council to protect land in this area against disfigurement by unsightly buildings, structures, or other development, by uncontrolled mineral workings, or by indiscriminate felling of trees, and to encourage, promote or enforce an improvement in the appearance of the land, buildings, or structures, which are unsightly, untidy, badly sited, or harmful in any way to the appearance or amenities in any part of the area. Development will not generally be permitted in the area, and the design and external appearance of that which may be approved, must be in sympathy with the landscape. Industry will not be permitted, unless natural to the area, and justified by very special circumstances.

Within this overall policy, two phases of development were envisaged. The first included housing and general infilling in those areas already earmarked (mainly north of the railway), additional shopping in Chalfont Station Road, a primary school, a girls' secondary school, and a car park. Some of these developments had already been started. Reservation of land for the diversion of the A404, and the preservation of approximately 1120 acres as an area of great landscape value, were also highlighted. In the second phase, covering up to 1974, twenty acres were allocated for houses, mainly at Chessfield Park.

The provision of a Little Chalfont by-pass was planned well before the last war, in that a route was identified, and no buildings were permitted on the land. The proposal was to divert the main road at a point opposite the Pineapple public house at Amersham Common, and then swing north across the railway line at the back of Boughtons. The by-pass would then cross Bell Lane, and run between the council estate and Beechwood Avenue, before crossing Chenies Avenue and Westwood Park, rejoining the original road at Stony Lane. The plan remained on the cards for over fifty years, until it was abandoned during the 1980s, and houses have now been built in Chenies Avenue and Bell Lane on part of the route. Some of the residents living in Beechwood Avenue in the 1950s were very concerned about the possible by-pass. They felt that they would be physically cut off from the rest of the village, and would also suffer from excessive traffic noise. To combat the latter, they clubbed together and planted a double row of conifers along the backs of the gardens on that side.

View taken in the 1950s, showing the newly constructed Oakington Avenue on the left.

View taken in 1993.

The growing population clearly needed more shopping and support facilities, and this need was met principally by the erecton of Chenies Shopping Parade in 1962. Until then, there had been an open field bounded by an old iron railing fence some four feet high. It was originally part of Loudhams Farm and was shown as an orchard on the Tithe Map of 1838. As late as the 1950s, ponies and donkeys used to graze there, and children would stroke and feed them while out shopping. To this day, the field behind the shops is known as The Donkey Field.

More shops were also built at Nightingales Corner, with infilling opposite the Village Hall, and between Lofts' hardware shop and the original Peter Pan's Parlour (now the electrical shop). The Travel Agent and the Fish shop, however, were not built until the late 1970s. Until then, there was an unkempt open space used, for a while, for storing building materials including drums of paint, at the rear of which stood a wooden shed used as a workshop. It was here that a fatal accident took place in March 1971, as reported in the local press:[33]

> FIRE EXPLOSION KILLS BYSTANDER
>
> A twenty-two year old sales representative was killed by an exploding oxygen cylinder while watching a fire at P.W. Motors, Burtons Lane on Friday. He was Mr. David Wilkins of Farnham. It is believed that he was watching the fire from about eighty feet when a cylinder exploded. It flew through the air, hit a tree and then struck Mr. Wilkins, carrying him twenty-five feet across the road. The fire broke out at 9.25am in a corrugated metal shed used as a workshop. The shed and a car inside were completely destroyed.

Amid this expansion of the shopping centre, the two old dwellings named Loudhams Cottages, standing on the site of the present village green, were still occupied. Sadly these reminders of by-gone times were finally demolished in 1967, in order to improve the vision splays for cars turning the corner. The village green was then created. Shortly afterwards, local traders complained that the Chenies Parade was somewhat isolated from the shops at Nightingales Corner and they suggested that the hedge surrounding the old cottage gardens should be cut much lower, thereby opening up the space between.

During the 1970s, considerable infilling took place between the White Lion Road and the railway line. The area which had originally been offered for sale by Lord Chesham in 1894 as desirable building land, was finally developed, with Clayton Walk, Beel Close, St. Nicholas Close, Kenway Drive, and Cumberland Close being built. Off Burtons Lane, new roads were created at Birkett Way, Park Grove and Garden Reach, and building in Long Walk was mainly completed.

A long-running saga involved the development of Shenstone House, which stood in large gardens in Cokes Lane by the entrance to the girls' school. Numerous applications were submitted for building various blocks of flats, the first one in 1974 for ninety residential units. After many planning refusals, a scheme for thirty-six flats was approved, and Snells Wood Court was built. Disagreements arose, however, when the contractor started felling many of the mature beech trees on the site, and this resulted in tree preservation orders being issued. These orders are still valid. As mentioned before, the dips in the ground on this property are reminders of the brick making industry which was carried on for at least one hundred and fifty years, until the turn of the century.

After the closure of Statters Switchgear in 1972, the site in the centre of the village became derelict and an eyesore. Outline plans were made for a new complex consisting of high-density housing, a supermarket, offices and light industry, but in 1978, it was announced that the District Council wished to acquire 3.7 acres of the site for sheltered homes for the elderly; shortly afterwards, Amersham International bought the remainder of the site, some four acres, for its new international headquarters. Work eventually started in the spring of 1983, and the new office was opened in September 1985. Almost immediately, a storm of protest broke out regarding its 'blue roof', many saying that it was completely out of character with the surroundings. Some even claimed that it had been chosen to match the colour of the nearby garage!

While the new offices were being built, Amersham International negotiated to purchase Pollards Wood, Bertram Mills' old home in Nightingales Lane. After his widow left in the 1940s, the house and grounds were taken over by the Imperial Cancer Institute, and were used for research over a period of thirty years. During the 1980s, Amersham International started to develop a new range of chemicals which did not involve the use of radioactive materials, and sought permission to construct a large laboratory in the grounds. Since the property lay in the green belt, and in a wholly residential district, planning permission was refused, and the matter was sent to appeal. After a five-day hearing in 1985, the Inspector ruled in favour of the proposal, on the grounds that the company was working in an important and advanced field, with a large proportion of its products being exported. The new laboratories were opened by Lord Young, then Minister of Trade and Industry, but there was a last-minute scare when a gale threatened to blow down the marquee which had been erected for the ceremony.

The homes for elderly people were completed late in 1985, and were named after Councillor Keith Halifax, who had campaigned for them over many years. He became Mayor of Amersham and was also well known as a founder member of the Little Chalfont Sports and Social Club, located in Elizabeth Avenue. The new homes have proved very popular, being conveniently located close to the shops. Climbing shrubs have been planted against the walls, which at first were somewhat bare, and are now beginning to cover the brickwork.

The latest development of any size is currently taking place on the site of the playing field in Elizabeth Avenue. Soon after the end of the last war, Major Boyce, who later became Chairman of Amersham Rural District Council, was instrumental in obtaining a large field from the Council at a nominal rent, in order to start a Sports and Social Club. This was in the 1950s at the time when the council estate was being built, and he felt it was important to retain an open space. The club, guided by Keith Halifax, expanded over the years, providing facilities for cricket, hockey and tennis, with a pavilion and bar for social events. It thrived for over thirty years until, in the late 1980s, the pavilion was burned down. The club, although insured, did not have sufficient funds to build a new one, and, in the end, accepted an offer from the District Council to move to a new site at Newlands Park, St. Giles. It was decided, however, to retain the tennis courts.

The District Council, who owned the land, felt that it could not be left as an open space, arguing that the larger sports ground at Westwood Park nearby could provide much better facilities. They proposed, therefore, that seventy-six houses and flats should be built for the Chiltern Hundreds Housing Association. Construction is now nearing completion, and the Housing Association is making available some of the dwellings on a 'shared equity' basis, thus helping first- time buyers who could not otherwise afford the whole costs initially.

Headquarters offices of Amersham International.

1955 view of Bedford Avenue and the Station taken from Elizabeth Avenue.
The National Benzole oil depot is on the right.

The "lake" in Elizabeth Avenue with boys and a sailing boat, taken in 1959.
Flooding was a regular occurrence until the road was made-up in the early 1960s.

Bedford Avenue in the foreground, with newly built bungalows in Elizabeth Avenue, taken in 1955. The field was well-known for mushrooms.

Lower Chenies Avenue taken from across the railway line, with the old signal box.

Taken in the late 1950s from an upstairs room in Lofts' Ironmongery.
The sharp bend in the road had just been smoothed out, and the "Donkey Field" with its iron railings shows up well on the right.

The Thames Bookshop and Peter Pans' Parlour.

Newly built shops in Chenies Parade in the early 1960s.
The old "Loudhams Cottages" can just be seen on the right.

Statter's site cleared ready for building Halifax House.

Schools and Churches

Before the start of the last war, the only schools in Little Chalfont were private, and children taking state education had to go either to Chenies or Amersham Common. The latter school was built in 1901 and enlarged in 1911 (although there is a reference in a newspaper[6] of 1892 to the National School at Amersham Common). For many years it was called the Amersham Common Elementary School (Mixed) and the buildings included the old Mission Church 'tin hut'. By 1919, there were 176 children on the roll, and the number increased to 303 by 1939. It is now St. George's Church of England School.

During the period between the wars, several small private schools were started. In 1925, Mademoiselle Camp announced that she visited and received pupils for French, German and English at 'Holne', a house in Village Way. The next year, Miss Grace Harvey established St. Nicholas as a Kindergarten and Junior School, firstly in a house in Loudhams Road, and finally in what is now St. Nicholas Close. Tuition fees were five guineas per term for the Kindergarten, six for Juniors and eight for Seniors over eleven years old. Lunch was one shilling per day. In a prospectus from the early 1930s, it states that 'the Principal will be at school to interview parents the whole day previous to the first day of each term'. The uniform for girls included a gym tunic in brown serge, a brown flannel blazer and overcoat, and a plain mauve tie. In summer the uniform was a brown and white gingham dress. Similarly for boys, the uniform consisted of brown flannel blazers and shorts, a brown overcoat and a cap with badge. Both indoor and outdoor shoes had to be brown, and the official school outfitter was Constance Glaze, who had a shop next to the telephone exchange. The school remained open for nearly forty years, often being used by local groups for evening meetings, until it was demolished to make way for a housing development in the grounds.

At the commencement of the war, Belle Vue School for girls was evacuated from Brondesbury, and transferred to 'Homestead', a large house in Burtons Lane. School fees for day pupils ranged from four to eight guineas per term, with children being taken up to the age of eighteen. Boarding fees were £30 per term, with laundry and medicine extra. Hot Bovril was available for six shillings and sixpence per term, and the girls could also take tennis or cricket lessons for fifteen shillings a term. The school maintained its own vegetable garden, and also had stables, with riding lessons costing two shillings and sixpence an hour. The uniform included a black blazer with gold trim, together with a blue and gold striped tie. Although the school catered only for girls, there is a school group photograph showing a lone boy. Apparently Mrs. Ruth Lelyveld's son could not be found a place at Chenies because of overcrowding by wartime evacuees, and so was sent to join the girls. Soon after the end of the war, Belle Vue moved to Hyde Heath.

Following the rapid population rise once building restrictions were lifted in the 1950s, the need for two new schools was identified and included in the Little Chalfont Development Plan. The first, Oakington Avenue County

Combined School, was opened on 10th January 1961, with Mr. Graham Jeremiah as headmaster, and catering for about three hundred children.

The next year, Dr. Challoner's High School for Girls was established in Little Chalfont, with 352 pupils and 24 teachers. It was officially opened in 1964 by Princess Marina, the Duchess of Kent, and to mark the occasion, the headmistress, Miss McMaster, quoted an extract from Sir John Hunt's book, 'The Ascent of Everest', saying: "There is always the moon to reach". She thus set a figurative target for successive generations of girls. Although the premises were new, the school itself had been part of Dr. Challoner's Grammar School in Amersham, which became co-educational in 1906. It had been founded in 1624 as a free grammar school in Amersham by Robert, a cousin of Sir Thomas Challoner, who was a tutor to Sir Robert Dudley, the Earl of Leicester. The girls' school now has 820 pupils, of whom 270 are in the 16-18 age group. It has a long and outstanding record of success, and continues to maintain its reputation for academic excellence. At GCSE level, about 95% of the pupils obtain grades A, B or C, which is double the national average; at Advanced Level, the pass rate is about 94%, half of which are at grades A or B. It is not surprising that, with such consistent results, the school is among the best in the country.

The third new school needed to cater for the post-war population boom was the Bell Lane Combined School, which was opened in September 1973, with Mr. Owen Williams as headmaster. It has places for over one hundred and fifty pupils, but is a little below that number at present, and is one of the few in Bucks to be purpose-built as a combined first and middle school. It has an active parent-teacher association which organises the annual Bell Lane Bonanza fete, raising several thousands of pounds each year.

The history of churches in Little Chalfont follows a pattern similar to that of the schools, in that services were held in private homes only until the mid-thirties. The Free Church conducted services and Sunday School at 'Meadow View', a wooden house in Bedford Avenue, situated at the foot of the bank which commuters used to scramble up and down on their way to and from the station. The name of the house was, of course, quite appropriate, since there was an open field directly opposite, stretching up the slope to Latimer (now Elizabeth) Avenue. The Catholic Church held Mass at 'Red Roofs', the home of Mr. Ferraro in Chenies Avenue, and also at 'Puck's Thatch' in Village Way, the home of Mrs. Angus-Yule. Other services were held in the early 1900s at 'The Roundhouse' in Nightingales Lane, and 'The White House' in Cokes Lane had its own private chapel, now converted into 'The White Cottage'.

The first church to be built was St. George's on the White Lion Road, which was opened, appropriately, on St. George's Day, 23rd April 1936, to replace the old St. Mary's Mission, formerly a pair of cottages occupied by railwaymen. The land was given for the erection of a permanent church, a clergy house and a parish hall. Mr. Geoffrey Lucas, the architect, designed the church in such a way that the central aisle could be built first, and the two side aisles later when funds permitted. The cost was £3500, of which some £1900 had been raised from weekly whist drives, and an annual bazaar. Collecting boxes were also distributed and returned on St. George's day each year. At the time, it was estimated that the addition of aisles on both sides would cost another £3000. A procession, which included a band, marched along the road to the church, where the Bishop of Buckingham conducted the dedication service. Access to the church from the main road was via a short wooden footbridge, which crossed a ditch at the side of the road, and through a pair of brick pillars.

In about 1950, the old wooden building which had housed Barclay's Bank next to the Sugar Loaves in the village was acquired and moved to the back of the church to provide a hall. Finally, in 1990, the 'Diamond Appeal' was launched to raise funds for a permanent hall, thus meeting the terms of the original trust. It was estimated that £125,000 would be needed, and one of the ways suggested for raising the money was to 'sell' bricks at £5 each. Building work was carried out in 1991, providing a brick hall along the west side of the existing church, which included a small meeting room. A separate entrance was made, allowing the hall to be used independently of the church.

Next to be built was the Methodist Church, which had started a Sunday School in the new Village Hall in October 1952, followed a month later by evening services. After only one year, the Sunday School had outgrown the Village Hall, and the works canteen of Statters was hired. In order to raise money for a permanent building, fêtes, equestrian shows, processions and baby shows were held, some in the grounds of Beel House, and these became quite a feature of village life. A plot of land was purchased in 1954 for £862 in Chalfont Avenue, and the foundation stone was laid by Revd. Leslie Henry on 22nd November 1958. Mr. Alick was the architect, Comben and Wakeling the builders, and the opening service was in July 1959.

The design was a dual-purpose one, with a sanctuary at one end which could be screened by sliding panels, and a stage at the other. Concerts were organised to raise more funds, including performances of The Mikado and The Messiah. Enlargements took place soon afterwards, and then in 1976, a large hall was built at the rear, named 'Newstead Hall' in memory of George and Ethel Newstead. For a while this hall was used by a local doctor to provide a limited medical service for the village. Present membership is about one hundred and thirty, and the church is very active with several group meetings taking place each day.

The third church to acquire a permanent building was St. Aidan's on the corner of Finch Lane and White Lion Road. In 1949, Father Tomlinson was appointed parish priest of Chesham Bois, and he became the driving force behind the development of the Catholic church. He set up a fund in 1958, and began the long and difficult search for a suitable site. Meanwhile the Village Hall was used for services, and on 9th April 1961, it was reported that one hundred and eight Easter Communions were held in the crowded hall; this prompted one gentleman to send a cheque for £50 towards the new church saying:

> I am desperately anxious to worship in a church again on Sundays before I die. I hope this cheque will help to bring forward just a little the commencement of your building operations.

While funds were being raised at Whitsun Fairs, jumble sales, dances, and performances by the Catholic Players, Father Tomlinson negotiated the purchase of the land at Finch Lane, paying only £1516. 10s, which he described as a 'miracle in this district'. (An acre of land had recently been auctioned for £118,000.) Mr. Hodsdon Archard was appointed architect, and in 1963 a contract was placed with Messrs. Abbiss and Hale of Rickmansworth, at a price of £28,198. The foundation stone was laid on 11th April 1964, and the first service was Midnight Mass at Christmas that year. Many of the present congregation remember the organising genius of Father Tomlinson, one of them saying: "He even had us paying for our pews!" The local Polish Community played a full role in contributing towards the new church, and they still conduct their own Mass every Sunday.

In March 1965, the Parish of St. Aidan Little Chalfont was established officially, with Father Leo Hammond as Parish Priest. The new presbytery had been completed, and the total building costs were about £40,000, all but £15,000 of which had been raised. Four years later, Monseigneur Gerard Collins, who was then Vicar-General of the Diocese of Northampton, took over at the church, making it known that he wished to become involved in parish affairs, rather than remaining in administration work. Father Collins, as he wished to be called, helped to clear all outstanding debts and to build a parish hall costing almost £40,000. Apart from his parish duties, he took a keen interest in local history, and, as mentioned, wrote a detailed article on the origins of Beel House. Ill health brought about his retirement in 1987, and he was followed by Father Ronald Bustin. Some problems have been experienced recently with cracks appearing in the church floor; since the pond in Finch Lane originally extended over a much wider area, it has been suggested that the ground adjacent to the church is still subject to settlement.

St. Nicholas School was demolished to make way for St. Nicholas Close.

Belle Vue School group in late 1939, showing Anthony Lelyveld as the only boy, on the left in the front row.

Raspberries were grown extensively at the side and rear of "Markham" on the White Lion Road. Local people helped pick the crop, and punnets were sent to markets in London.

An outing for the Little Chalfont Brownies in 1950.

Mr. Bowler the village chimney sweep.
The pond in Finch Lane was originally quite large. Taken about 1924.

The pond often froze in winter, and people would come with skates.

A scene in Finch Lane.

White Lion Road in the early 1960s, almost clear of traffic.

Miscellany

Mention has been made of the small group of cottages in Finch Lane at the time of the Tithe Map survey in 1838. Blacksmiths were listed there at that time, and again in the 1861 Census. Chair makers, lace makers and straw plaiters were also listed in addition to a carpenter. Mr. James Bowler, the chimney sweep, was another tradesman who lived there for many years, and his daughter, Mrs. Phyllis Harriss, recalls that he went on his rounds with a small horse-drawn cart. At the end of each day, the cart was left at the front of the cottage, while the horse was turned loose in the back garden. Because of the nature of his job, Mr. Bowler suffered from a dry throat, and thus needed to call into the White Lion Inn several times a day in order to ease the problem. His wife, Hettie Rose, and her mother before her, contributed to the family income by laying out the dead, even if this meant turning out in the middle of the night with a lantern. As a child at the turn of the century, Hettie used to wander off to the brick works in Cokes Lane to play with the wet clay.

A sad accident took place in June 1935, when George Harris, an uncle of Phyllis, was killed when a steam engine belonging to Grovers ran out of control as he was driving down Bell Lane. In trying to stop, her uncle steered the engine into the steep bank at the side of the lane, but this caused it to overturn. He died later that day from severe burns caused by escaping steam. Phyllis herself recalls picking wild raspberries in the woods along the main road; and also that a bomb exploded one night in the air above Finch Lane, and that her father kept a piece of shrapnel as a memento. She also states that the pond in Finch Lane, which nowadays is small and often dry, was several times larger and always full when she was a child in the 1920s. During hard winters, people used to skate there. Finch Lane also had its own shop, a general store, which was in the front room of Mrs. Eliza Woolhead's cottage.

In 1842 there was an exchange of land[34] with the Hon. C C Cavendish (later Lord Chesham) whereby the Duke of Bedford gave up Dell Farm and its fourteen acres, in return for Old House Farm and thirty-two acres lying between the farm and the Sheep Houses. A note attached to a survey document states:

> This estate shows little or no improvement on the value previous to 1831, nor will it ever do much more, for it is a naturally hungry and ungrateful soil, and does not make such a return as to tempt men to farm it highly.

The situation has not changed to any marked extent during the intervening one hundred and fifty years, the land still being regarded as hard, stony and not particularly productive.

Mention was made earlier of the Nathaniel Snell Charity dating from 1684, but this was not the only one involving the parish of Amersham. Among many others, the largest was set up in the 1890s, when the Tyrwhitt Drake family of

Aerial photograph of Little Chalfont, taken by Ronald Mitchell in 1993.

Amersham gave Burtons Farm with one hundred and eighty acres to the Almshouse Charity. In March 1913, the trustees of these various charities decided to combine them into the Amersham United Charities under a single board, thus amalgamating the sums of money into more worthwhile amounts for local causes. In May 1921, the trustees decided to dispose of Burtons Farm, putting it up for auction at the Railway Hotel in Amersham, where it fetched £8,600.

Many residents have contributed anecdotes from earlier times, and the following are a selection of them:

The area around the station was renowned for excellent mushrooms, in particular between Bedford and Elizabeth Avenue, and near Oakington Avenue.

Miss Ivy Wheeler remembers Mr. Chapman, one of the founders of the local garage, driving along the White Lion Road from his home in Amersham Common, to the station where he operated a taxi service. He used to crack his whip at children on their way to school near the Black Horse bridge, pretending to frighten them. Sometimes, as a change, he would blow an old trumpet.

Before Oakington Avenue had been extended through to the main road, residents from the far end next to Lodge Lane used to take a short cut to the station by crossing Farmer Simpson's field, where the school is now situated. To counter this, he grazed some bulls and later ploughed the field. But the commuters were not deterred; they carefully made their way along the edge of the field next to the railway line. In the early 1950s, The Retreat, a small cul-de-sac off Oakington Avenue, consisted of only two or three bungalows, and every November, the central grass area would be taken over for bonfires and fireworks. Also in the fifties, there was a proposal to build a cinema in Oakington Avenue.

Staying at this end of the village, it is worth noting that the short stretch between the main road and the end of Oakington Avenue, now a section of Church Grove, was once known as Stony Lane, part of the road to Latimer. Three generations or so ago, the area near the junction of Stony Lane and the main road was known as Four and Twenty Ashes.

Mr. Payne from Nightingales Farm supplied fresh milk seven days a week from a handcart carrying milkchurns from which he filled his customer's jugs, using the appropriate measure from the selection of shining metal cups which hung along the side of the cart. His round was eventually bought by Express Dairies in about 1957. A close neighbour of his in Burtons Lane was Mrs. Thyra Baird, who lived at Pucks Paigles. A somewhat eccentric lady, she was devoted to the animals which she had around the house. It is said that she kept more than a hundred geese, and knew the name of each one. She built a puppet theatre in an old wooden shed,[27] and entertained local children with shows; the hut was only removed in the 1980s.

The approach to the station from the village was only constructed in the early thirties, and remained a private road for many years. In order to maintain the private ownership, a length of string was stretched across the entrance once a year. The row of shops were originally of temporary construction, rented on short-term leases only, so that they could be pulled down in order to widen the railway track and platform. A taxi service was once operated by Grovers on the Bedford Avenue side of the station, and according to one story, passengers would throw small stones onto the tin roof of the taxi shelter in order to call a driver.

Before cars became widely used, workers at Statters Switchgear factory used to arrive by rail from towns such as Chesham, Amersham and Rickmansworth, bringing their bicycles with them. Mornings and evenings, swarms of them would crowd the short stretch of road to and from the station.

Mr. Berkley, at the butcher's shop on the corner of Cokes Lane, once applied for permission to build a slaughter house at the back of the premises. This was not agreed, but a little later on, the afternoon Women's Institute was given permission to donate and erect a clock above the shop. The shop frontage was originally decorated with blue and white tiles which surrounded the butcher's name.

Harewood Downs golf club was created at the beginning of the century, following a complicated series of land purchases. It was restricted to Members of Parliament and the legal profession. On Friday afternoons, when 'the House' had finished its business for the week, parties of MPs would travel to Rickmansworth, and then by horse-drawn coach to the golf club. The name Harewood Downs is believed to be a modern corruption of Harrow Downs.[35]

Between the wars, pomegranates were sold for one penny at Hoare's Bell Lane Stores, and fresh fish was available from the garage at the side. Before the shop was built, fish and vegetables were sold from a van with a large tarpaulin which parked on the corner of Bell Lane and the main road.

Before the last war, the Rendezvous used to provide a limited library service to residents, and books could be borrowed for a penny. After the war, the Thames Book Shop was opened next to Peter Pan's Parlour by Lady KirkPatrick, offering stationery goods and a library. A voluntary library centre was also provided in the Village Hall, run for many years by Mrs. Beryl Thorne until her retirement in 1959. A fire once broke out in the library, scattering burnt pages about the village. Eventually the little library room became quite inadequate, and a new building was erected in 1974. It cost £18,838 including all internal furniture, and care was taken in siting it to avoid losing any of the mature trees nearby. The library is now a well-used and vital facility in the village.

Mr. Ned Aldin recalled that when the beech woods were being felled during the war, he was able to buy coils of surplus timber for only seven shillings and sixpence. He also used to shoot rooks, which his wife made into rook pies.

Mrs. Creighton, at Peter Pan's Parlour, related how, in the early days, a customer would come into the shop on a morning to choose a dress; Mrs. Creighton would then travel to a wholesaler in London that afternoon and deliver the dress the next morning.

Finally Mr. Haddon's words, written when over eighty years old, seem to sum up the feelings of many people who enjoy living in the village:

> It is a long way from the time when I was a schoolboy, and we rode our bicycles from old Amersham. I came to Little Chalfont in 1970 and it took me a little time to adjust, but now I think it was the best thing I ever did. Old Amersham is now full of strangers, but Little Chalfont is a very pleasant and convenient area, and I have many good friends. We have our Post office, our bank and really there is no need to go out of the village for anything.

Chenies Parade shopping centre, built in 1962.

Barn at Beel House Nurseries.

The wooden frame is thought to be an Elizabethan window, which connected the living room of the cottage to the adjacent cattle shed.

Taxi service at the station in the early 1930s, looking towards Elizabeth Avenue.

Only cyclists are in sight along the White Lion Road in the early 1950s.

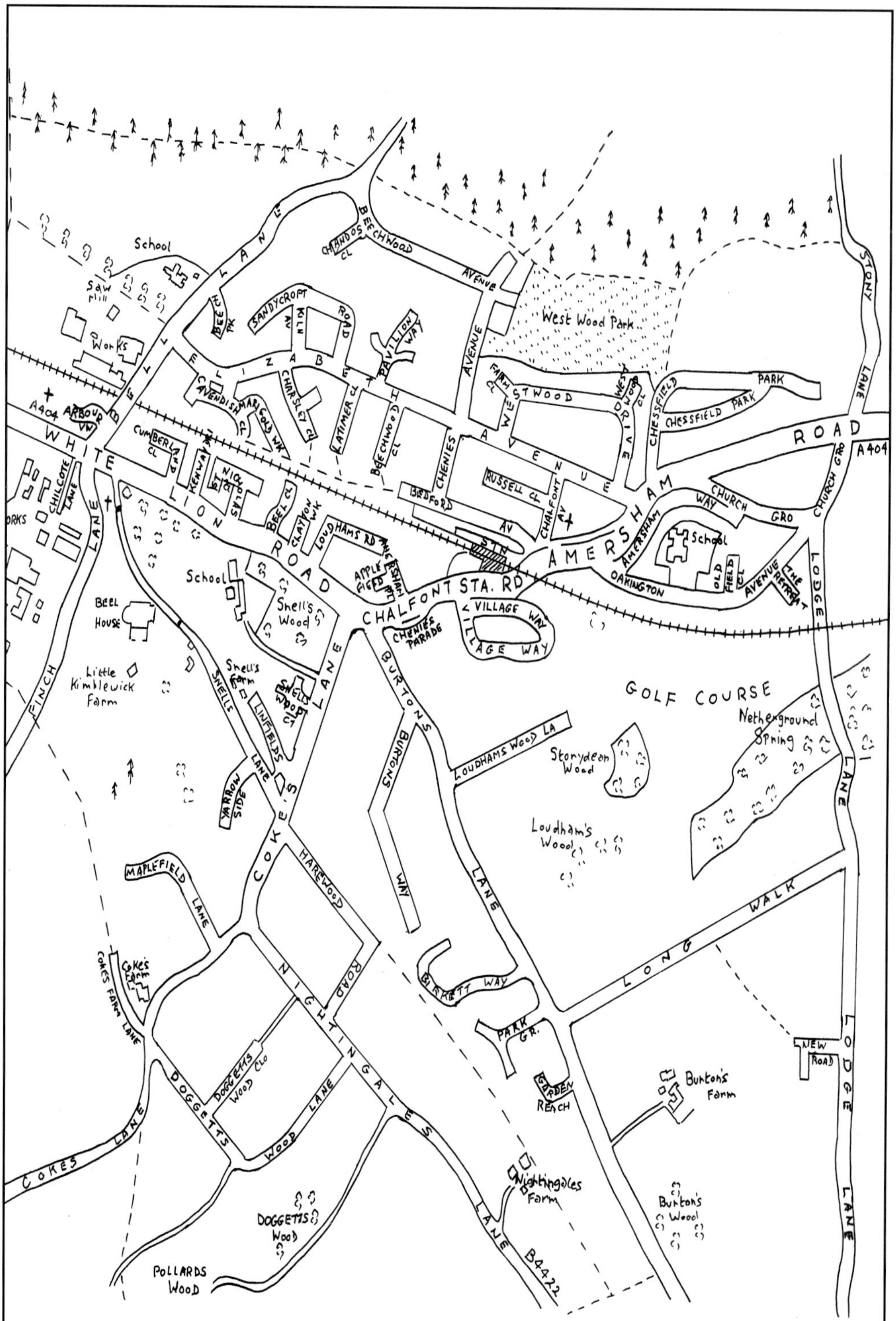

Present day map of Little Chalfont.
Based on the 1991 Ordnance Survey 1:10,000 map with the permission of the Controller of Her Majesty's Stationary Officer, © Crown Copyright.

Little Chalfont Rural Preservation Society

The Society was founded in 1960 in order to fight a proposed development on green belt land near Long Walk, and it is perhaps an illustration of the influence it has had on local matters that the land in question remains an open area today. The objectives of the Society are to preserve the character of the area and its surroundings, to protect the distinct identity of the district, and to ensure that developments are in keeping with its rural character. It is open to all who support these objectives, and membership numbers have been maintained at above one thousand for several years. There are two main strands to the Society's work: that of monitoring planning applications and developments, and that of improving the visual appearance of the village.

On planning matters, objections are only lodged if it felt that a proposal would be out of character with the surroundings. This is sometimes a question of design, but much more often it relates to matters of high-density over-development. Since the Society is careful to object only when important issues are involved, its views are respected, and the District Council frequently supports them.

During the last few years, the Society has instigated a programme of improvements in the village. Flowering trees have been planted in the grass verges near the shopping centre and on the village green, and a much-admired raised border of miniature conifers and winter-flowering heathers has been constructed near the green. The Society is grateful for the support it received in this latter project from a major local company. In addition, well over two tons of daffodils have been planted from one end of the village to the other. Crocuses and snowdrops have been massed on the green, and bluebells have recently been planted in Snells Wood. It is hoped that further schemes will be undertaken as and when funds allow.

When the proposal to write a History of Little Chalfont started to make progress, the Society decided to publish the book itself rather than turn to a commercial company. To assist with funding, members and local residents were invited to sponsor the book by way of paying advance deposits, and considerable support has been received. The Society is grateful for this, and the names of all sponsors are inscribed within.

Sources

1. Bedford C.R.O. R1/189/2
2. Bucks County Development Plan 1964
3. Records of Bucks. Vol 16
4. Bucks C.R.O. "The Home of the Penningtons"
5. Bucks C.R.O. IR/12 BR
6. Bucks Free Press Aug 1892
7. "Latimer" by Keith Branigan C.V.A.H.S.
8. Title Deeds - Houses in Burtons Way
9. Bucks C.R.O. D/CH/A 738
10. Amersham Reference Library
11. Statute 2 & 3 PH. & Mary C8
12. British Library
13. County Reference Library Aylesbury
14. Rickmansworth Reference Library
15. Bucks Archaeological Society . BAS 501/34
16. Title Deeds
17. Act of Parliament 55 GEOIII 1815
18. Bucks Brickmakers - Aylesbury Ref Library
19. Pigot's Directory 1830
20. House of Commons R.O.
21. Bedford C.R.O.
22. Greater London R.O. Acc 1297/MET 1/16
23. Greater London R.O. Acc 1297/MET 10/403
24. London Transport Museum
25. Greater London R.O. Acc 1297/MET 10/673
26. Bedford C.R.O. R Box 329
27. Christopher North - Private Papers
28. Bucks Examiner Dec 1922
29. Bucks Examiner Nov 1936
30. "Steam in the Veins" - John Boughton
31. British Telecom Archives
32. Bucks Examiner Nov 1952
33. Bucks Examiner Mar 1971
34. Bedford C.R.O. R5/1842
35. Article on Harewood Downs by Gary May

PICTURES, MAPS AND DRAWINGS–ACKNOWLEDGMENTS

Frances Ashdown: *65, 68, 74 upper, 77 lower, 90 lower, 109 lower.* Aylesbury Reference Library: *29.* The Author: *15 upper, 19 lower, 24 lower, 36 lower, 37 lower, 38 lower, 39 lower, 40 lower, 41 lower, 42 lower, 44, 100 lower, 103 lower, 124, 126.* Berkshire Records Office: *Front end papers.* Bucks Archaeological Society: *32.* Bucks County Museum: *24 upper, 36 upper, 37 Upper, 38 Upper, 39 upper, 40 upper, 41 upper, 42 Upper, 47 upper.* Bucks Record Office: *17, 32.* Ray Edmunds: *80, 85 lower, 86 upper.* George Hance: *2.* Phyllis Harriss: *25 upper.* Christopher Hojsgaard: *48.* Anne Hearn: *86 lower.* LCRPS: *9, 10 lower, 12 upper, 15 lower, 19 upper, 26 lower, 58 upper, 63, 73 lower, 84 lower, 85 upper, 107, 108, 110 lower, 117 upper.* Ruth Lilyweld: *115 lower.* David Lofts: *74 lower, 109 upper.* London Transport Museum: *53, 57 lower, 58 lower, 64.* Alec Mead: *82.* Ronald Mitchell: *120.* Leslie Myerscough: *116 lower.*Christopher North: *61, back end papers.* Rickmansworth Reference Library: *31.* Dudley Rhodes: *95 upper.* Colin Seabright: *8 upper, 10 upper, 11, 12 lower, 25 lower, 26 upper, 47 lower, 56, 57 upper, 71, 73 upper, 95 lower, 96, 103 upper, 110 upper, 115 upper, 118, 125 lower.* Mrs Sexton: *117 lower.* Majorie Simpson: *Drawing on cover, 4, 23, 35, 46, 55, 70, 94, 99, 106, 123.* Gladys Swain: *116 upper.* Nancy Thomas: *90 upper.* Deirdre White: *110 upper.* Doreen Wright: *72.*

Sponsors

1 J.R. Wickison
2 K.M. Hilton
3 Mrs A.D. White
4 Betty Price
5 George Wainwright
6 Jean Wainwright
7 Charlotte Peters
8 Sarah Peters
9 Christopher Edwards
10 Carolyn M. Chaventre
11 Robin C. Chaventre
12 Mr & Mrs D. Witton
13 Cheryl Gillan MP
14 Jack Leeming
15 A.T. Weatherill
16 Leslie & Frieda Jones
17 Julie Wolstenholme
18 Paul Hodsdon Archard
19 Mrs Joan Daniell
20 Mrs Pat Baker
21 Sue Beresford
22 John Harrison
23 Mr Robert Snell
24 Mrs Ros Snell
25 Eric L. George
26 Leslie & Martin Totty
27 J.E. Schneider
28 Mr & Mrs R.A.A. Hepworth
29 Mr & Mrs L. Brodie
30 Mr & Mrs J.A. Paine
31 Mr A.E.J. Yelland
32 Mr & Mrs J. Maley
33 Marjorie Simpson
34 Bernard Simpson
35 Sarah & Philip Miles
36 J.V. Adams
37 R.S. Adams
38 Mrs D.M. Lloyd
39 Mrs D.E. Johnson
40 Miss K.M. Brayne
41 M.C. Carrington
42 F.D. Fowler
43 Mrs Kathleen Montey
44 Mrs S. Gradidge
45 Mr & Mrs M.J. Biles
46 Mrs S.M. & Mr C.B. Russell
47 Mr D.N. Fogden
48 Mr D.N. Fogden
49 Mr D.N. Fogden
50 Mr & Mrs D.E. Lovett
51 Mr & Mrs S. Bunker
52 Mr J.S. Allen
53 Gordon & Pat Milne
54 C.S. Repton
55 Mr & Mrs J. Wong
56 D.C. Howroyd
57 W & M.E. Troth
58 Richard Salter
59 Mr J.R. Hope
60 Dr Victor Freeman
61 Mr & Mrs Mills
62 Mr & Mrs L.A. Davis
63 N.P. & L.F.M. Cutcliffe
64 F.R. Fielden
65 Mrs J.E. Dabinett
66 Mr & Mrs T.F. Phillips
67 E.T. Phillips
68 A.D. Phillips
69 M.A.J. Phillips
70 Mr & Mrs L.J. Woodman
71 Alan Stuart Harris
72 John & Pam Tallyn
73 Mary & Nicholas Lines
74 Mary & Nicholas Lines
75 Jim & Margaret Hedger
76 Michael & Drina Parker
77 Mr & Mrs A.J. Reid
78 Mrs P. Lancaster
79 Mrs P. Lancaster
80 David Roll
81 Mr & Mrs Howard Pountney
82 Mr & Mrs R Buck
83 Andrew & Julie Gorrie
84 J.B. Sargent
85 Nigel & Irene Spoor
86 Desmond Gray
87 Mr & Mrs C.B. Adamson
88 Mr E.H. & Miss G.F. Foster
89 Gea & Paul Covell
90 Ivan A. Duck
91 Mr & Mrs V.T.M.R. Tenison
92 Mr & Mrs C. Pritchard
93 Mr W.V. Fleet
94 Mrs Joan M. Jones
95 David Johnston
96 Mr & Mrs C.E. Vincent
97 Mr & Mrs K.C. Clarke
98 Hazel Baker
99 Miss A.E. Kempster
100 Mr & Mrs A.P. Jones
101 Mr & Mrs J.H. & J.E. Holmes
102 Mr & Mrs J.R. & D.L. Payne
103 Mr & Mrs J.R. & D.L. Payne
104 Mrs Marjorie I. Penton
105 Mr & Mrs J. Stacey
106 Mr & Mrs D.W. Cordell
107 Sandra & Michael Bralsford
108 Kevin & Helen Beaumont
109 Mr & Mrs R.A. Wall
110 D. Gane
111 John & Mary Stoyle
112 P. Weeks

113 Gordon Ross
114 A.F. Macleod Matthews
115 J.D. Coombe
116 Robert & Audrey Payne
117 Mr B.M. Ashdown
118 Mrs F.M. Ashdown
119 Mrs L. Martin
120 Mr & Mrs J. Chadwick
121 Robert & Jean Cotton
122 Mr & Mrs R.C. Roe
123 Mr & Mrs B. Richards
124 Roger Griffin
125 Mr R. Wentworth
126 Mr & Mrs F.H. Barker-Benfield
127 Stanley J. Crockett
128 Mr Robert L. Tayler
129 R.S. Little
130 Mrs P.A. Kelly
131 Guy & Susan Newman
132 K.E. Hall
133 John Naylor-Smith
134 Eileen Cheshire
135 Mr & Mrs L. Pollard
136 Mr A.H.W. & Mrs D.O. Kennard
137 Mr R.A. Duparc
138 Mr Gordon Gibson
139 Mr & Mrs A.C. Blackburn
140 Caroline Ann Hutt
141 David Russell Hutt
142 Robert & Phyllis Plowright
143 Mrs B.J.S. Rodgers
144 Ian Ainsley
145 Mrs I.D. Cooley
146 Mr & Mrs D.J. Blowfield
147 Keith E.O. Smith
148 Mr & Mrs C. Hogbin
149 Mrs Jean Britton
150 John Brooks
151 Mr & Mrs G.S. MacGill
152 Mr & Mrs G.D. Swetman
153 Mr & Mrs E.J. Taylor
154 Mrs S.B. Churchill
155 Nigel & Ann Aylesbury
156 Peter Martin
157 Stewart Walker & Deborah Ball
158 Mrs M.A. Burrows
159 Mrs M.A. Burrows
160 N.J. & L. Smyth
161 Colin G. Grimsey
162 Gill Grimsey
163 Mr & Mrs J. Hinkly
164 Mr & Mrs J. Hinkly
165 A.A. & J. Darbyshire
166 Mrs Joyce Bradford
167 Mr George Norwich
168 Dr & Mrs W.E.H. Cockle
169 Miss R. Whitmore
170 Dr & Mrs W.M. Dixon
171 Mr & Mrs G. Harman
172 J.G. Curtis
173 J. & B. Henderson
174 Mrs K.G. Crayford
175 Mr & Mrs T.H. Fowler
176 Mr & Mrs P.A. Chapman
177 J. Weston
178 A.F. & S.M. Winder
179 M.G. & D.I. Jones
180 Mrs G. Birch
181 Mr D.W. & Mrs C.P. Taylor
182 Mr & Mrs T.R. Ball
183 Mr E. Clifton
184 Terry Ryder
185 W.T.B. Lewis
186 Miss Carol Mead
187 Colin Seabright
188 J.L.W. Oliver
189 P.G. Wotton
190 Mr & Mrs Colin Charlton
191 Mrs A.S. Curry
192 Mr & Mrs P. Bollinghaus
193 T.M. Bradfield
194 K.A. Reynolds
195 Ian & Leslie Mathieson
196 R.M. Scott
197 Kenneth C. Walker
198 D.H. Crampton
199 Mr & Mrs Michael Whiteley
200 Mr & Mrs Francis Flynn
201 Mr C.J. Cooper
202 David Provan
203 Ronald Mitchell
204 Lady Leslie Kirkpatrick
205 Christopher North
206 Phyllis & Jolyon Lea
207 John S. Jordan
208 Mr & Mrs D.A. Rudd
209 Mr C.N. Rudd
210 Mrs J.A. Bradley
211 Mr & Mrs A. Page
212 Mr & Mrs M. Frazier
213 Mr & Mrs M. Frazier
214 Neil & Olive Frazer
215 Richard B. Sykes
216 Mrs M. Leven
217 Mrs R.F. Smith
218 Ronald R. Collins
219 J. Langford Stacey
220 Suzanne & Gordon Simpson
221 Gillian S. Mansfield
222 Brian D.F. Mansfield
223 John & Sarah Watkins
224 Mr & Mrs K.N. Baffoe

225 R.G. Biggs
226 Capt & Mrs G.A. Ramsden
227 Capt & Mrs G.A. Ramsden
228 Richard & Sue Prime
229 Mrs Anne Roques
230 M. Noble
231 J & M. Hynes
232 Mr & Mrs A.A. Clark
233 Mr H. Wilcock
234 Sylvia Webb
235 Deanna Pearce
236 G.W. Page
237 Rosemary Smith
238 Miss N.G. Melville
239 Mr & Mrs B. Symes
240 David & Marilyn Smith
241 Mr F.T. Short
242 Hilda & Frank Longdon
243 Mrs Margaret A. Carey
244 Keith E. Fletcher
245 Mr & Mrs R. Nicklin
246 Mr A.D. Manecki
247 Mr & Mrs P. Mossman
248 Guy & Hannah Ruddock
249 Mrs Raffaelle Cuming
250 Anne & Peter Mills
251 Mr & Mrs Arnott
252 Adrian & Jane Lamb
253 Andrew J.K. Chatterton
254 Anthony C.R. Chatterton
255 Michael W.H. Cohn
256 David & Margaret Thorpe
257 Julie & Keith Lowe
258 Robert & Mary Lawson
259 Dorothy Thomson
260 Mr & Mrs G.L. Stephens
261 Mr & Mrs B.A. Walsh
262 John & Chris Philipps
263 R.D. West
264 Mrs Peggy Palmer
265 Christy Matthews
266 Jean C. & J.M. Daniel
267 Mrs Joanna Poynton
268 Jessica Richardson
269 Dorothy & Brian Drew
270 Mr & Mrs E.J.M. Pugh
271 Mr & Mrs G. Marshall-Taylor
272 Julie & Rod Bungey
273 A.G. Gage
274 David & Jackie German
275 Mr & Mrs G.L. Jenkins
276 Mr & Mrs I.B. Paterson
277 J.J. Russell
278 John Jenkins
279 Graham Blunden
280 Zena Sutcliffe
281 Mrs J.L. Luthert
282 Mr L.P.T. Pate
283 Philip & Linda Edwards
284 John & Mavis Warner
285 Ida Kinch
286 Chris & Mike Gunnell
287 Mr & Mrs David M. Ingram
288 Mr & Mrs V. Clark
289 D. Townend
290 Betty & Derek Taylor
291 Mr & Mrs H.R. Goold
292 Joan & Tony Caparn
293 Mrs Joyce Collins
294 Kathleen Christensen
295 Mr & Mrs G.W.R. Beckley
296 Mrs M. & Mr R.J. Banks
297 M.E. Howard
298 Dr Challoner's Grammar School
299 Mr & Mrs D. Ball
300 W.B.G. Collis
301 Miss W.G. Bannister
302 Arthur & Marian Ainsworth
303 I.G. Mackay
304 Mr P.F. Howard
305 Patricia D. Tutin
306 Alan & Christine Clarke
307 Mr P.H.G. Passfield
308 Miss Mary Wyeth
309 Mr & Mrs C. Sigger
310 Martin & Mig Keys
311 Helen & Ian Comley
312 David Lewis
313 Mr & Mrs G.C. Stafford
314 T. Morrissey
315 David Lofts
316 Mr A. & Mrs A.S. King
317 Lyndsay Hall
318 Mr & Mrs G.J. Hayes
319 Mr P.J. & Mrs J. Aley
320 R. Lewis Booth
321 Jim Brooks
322 Christine Brooks
323 Karen Brooks
324 Catherine Brooks
325 Mrs M. Johnston
326 Paul Reynolds
327 Andrew Greenwood
328 Mr & Mrs R.D. Sankey
329 Mr & Mrs K. Hardwick
330 Mr F.H. Shortt
331 Richard E. Bradley
332 John & Carolyn Phillips
333 Mrs C.B. Taylor
334 Mrs C.B. Taylor
335 Mrs C.M. Letham
336 Sally & Mark Elderfield

337 Hamza & Farida Ali
338 Mr & Mrs H.B.T. McLaren
339 Mrs S. Singh
340 Mrs Gillian Mansfield
341 Mr W.E. Lloyd
342 T.D. Glover
343 Mr & Mrs H.V. Pugh
344 R. Archer
345 P.L. Gray
346 Mrs R. Woolon
347 B.D. & M.E. Treharne
348 Mr G.W. Dolitzscher
349 The Clarksons
350 Mr & Mrs D. Redmayne
351 Miss Phillipa Skock
352 Mrs Jennifer & Mr Edward Hayward
353 A.H. Bayley
354 P. Marston
355 M.H. & R.M. Shanahan
356 Mrs S.M. Humby
357 V.M. Roberts
358 E.R. Whithear
359 Mr D.S.M. Nussbaum
360 Mrs K.M. Nussbaum
361 Mr D.W. Riddoch
362 Mrs B.T. Riddoch
363 Mr F.P. Wilkinson
364 Kenneth Howard
365 Mrs B. Brightley
366 Miss J. Wilkerson
367 Mrs Anna Wood
368 Mr Alexander Wood
369 Betty Mitchell
370 Miss Lyn Gilbert & Mr Michael Miller
371 Mr & Mrs G. Webb
372 Mrs P. Benstead
373 Mr & Mrs Alan Turner
374 Mr & Mrs J. Hall
375 Jan Leszczynski
376 J.M. Learmont
377 Barbara Wootton
378 Colin Jones
379 F.W. Sturch
380 Mrs A.M. Thomas
381 Mr & Mrs A.R. Lawson
382 Miss Rosemary Berkerey
383 Mrs E. Button
384 Mrs J.M. Allday
385 P.H. Cresswell
386 Mrs H.M. Pickles
387 Barbara Swoffer
388 G.R. Hance
389 Kenneth & Christine Coppock
390 Mr & Mrs S.A. Prime
391 Mr & Mrs S.A. Prime
392 Mrs C.M. Roberts
393 A.M. Gray
394 G. De Barra
395 Mr & Mrs T.J. Hunt
396 R.W. Boughton
397 R.W. Boughton
398 R.W. Boughton
399 B.J. Fletcher
400 Helen Tyers
401 Rita & Alan Boardman
402 Mr Geoffrey T. Hewson
403 Mrs K. & Mr D. Dawson
404 Mr & Mrs L.T. Anthony
405 Mr M.A. France
406 Mrs L. Deuters
407 D.A. Kerr
408 D.A. Kerr
409 Judy and Christian Hosjgaard
410 Mrs Wendy Coventry
411 P.L. O'Curry
412 Mrs D. Chaney
413 Miss I.E. Wheeler
414 Mr & Mrs N.J. Hamilton
415 G.J. Gibson
416 Ian & Julie Ferris
417 Miss Christine Anne Gibbs
418 Mr & Mrs F.W. Haines
419 H. Lang
420 Robert A.E. Hazell
421 Mr D.H. Grice
422 Peta & Nigel Norman
423 H. Schlenzig
424 Councillor Peter & Mrs Penny Mullins
425 Councillor Peter & Mrs Penny Mullins
426 Councillor Peter & Mrs Penny Mullins
427 Mr & Mrs J. Barber
428 Graham & Janine Page
429 Mr & Mrs John Barker
430 Mr V.R. Podbury
431 Miss Therese Byrne
432 Mrs E. Syms
433 Mrs S.M. Humby
434 Mr & Mrs R.J. Tweed
435 M.H. & L.E. Williams
436 Kernneth Saunders
437 Trevor & Quita Knibb
438 Anonymous
439 Anonymous
440 Anne Marshall
441 Mr Robin A. Eddy
442 Sharon F. Poch
443 Charlotte Ryman
444 James Ryman
445 Frances White
446 Roger White
447 Duncan White

Dates

1600 'The Piece' thought to have been built by this time.
1646 Thomas Russell captured at Loudhams Farm.
1684 Charity founded by Samuel Snell.
1708 Beale House sold by John Pennington.
1739 Grimsdell's Tomb erected.
1763 John Rocque's Map.
1768 Act of Parliament authorised the Turnpike Road.
1769 Kender Mason bought Beel House.
1770 Thomas Jefferys' map shows turnpike gate.
1774 Brick kiln near Snells Farm.
1790 John Cary's map shows turnpike gate.
1796 Sheephouses built as a blacksmith's shop.
1800 Map of Beel House Estate shows Beel Lodge.
1816 Amersham Common enclosure.
1820 By this date, the road through Beel House Estate had been closed, and Cokes Lane created.
1822 Milestone manufactured by John Wilder of Reading.
1830 White Lion Inn listed in trade directory.
1836 Beel House purchased by William Lowndes.
1838 Tithe map produced.
1858 Half of Snells Farm sold to Margaret Mair.
1859 Vicar of Latimer writes about Grimsdell's Tomb.
1881 Hatfield-Reading Turnpike Road closed.
1888 White Lion Inn extended for railway workers. Station called Chalfont Road at request of St. Giles Parish Council.
1889 Horse-drawn carriages introduced to provide a service from the staion to Amersham and Chalfont St.Giles. Metropolitan railway reached Chalfont Road and Chesham.
1892 Amersham Common School treat at Beel House Park.
1894 Lord Chesham offers land for sale along main road. Land bought by the Duke of Bedford to stop building development.
1897 Boughtons founded as makers of agricultural machinery.
1904 Land for Harewood Downs golf course purchased.
1910 Pullman cars introduced on Met line.
1915 Name of station changed to Chalfont and Latimer.
1920 Duke of Bedford sold land along the main road for building development. 'Village Way' land sold to G H & J W Darvell and C Jeffs on 29 Sept. Statter Switchgear founded.
1921 Council houses built on corner of Bell Lane. Burtons Farm sold by Amersham United Charities.
1922 Howard Freeborn starts building houses in Village Way, then called Chalfont Station Village.

1925 Name of village changed to Little Chalfont. Oxford Stores and the Rendezvous built. Statter Switchgear move to main site.

1926 White Lion Road widened. Amersham Road constructed to by-pass Church Grove. St. Nicholas School opened. Munn & Chapman founded.

1927 Path constructed from station to steps by main road. Oil lamps provided at the station. Three electric lights installed in Village way. Larger waiting room built at the station.

1930 Telephone exchange with operators opened in the Post Office.

1933 Station Approach built to provide access to the station from the village.

1935 Duke of Bedford sold 30 acres of land for building development; this later became Amersham Way, Church Grove and Oakington Avenue.

1936 St.George's church dedicated.

1937 Automatic telephone exchange opened.

1939 Pullman car service terminated. Bertram Mill's circus animals moved to Pollards Wood.

1940 Radiochemical centre started. Belle-Vue School moved from London to Burtons Lane. Wooden hut donated for the Home Guards; became the old village hall.

1944 Two bombers crashed on outskirts of village.

1946 Afternoon Women's Institute formed.

1948 Radiochemical houses built.

1950 Old village hall burned down. Council houses in Elizabeth Avenue started.

1951 Snells Wood purchased by Amersham R D C.

1952 Present village hall opened.

1953 Latimer Avenue changed to Elizabeth Avenue to mark the Queen's Coronation.

1956 Little Chalfont Sports Club founded with 366 members.

1959 Methodist Church building dedicated.

1960 Little Chalfont Sports Club opened by the Duke of Edinburgh. Little Chalfont Rural Preservation Society founded.

1961 Steam engines withdrawn from the railway and replaced by 'Silver' electric carriages. Oakington Avenue School opened.

1962 Dr. Challoner's High School for Girls opened. Chenies Parade shopping centre built.

1964 Houses started in St. Nicholas Close. Little Chalfont Town Map published.

1965 St.Aidan's Catholic Church dedicated.

1967 Village green created.

1972 Statter Switchgear closed.

1973 Bell Lane School opened.

1974	New library built.
1975	Railway bridge replaced.
1976	Trees planted opposite end of Elizabeth Avenue.
1978	Trees planted in shopping parade for Silver Jubilee.
1982	Rose bed removed on village green.
1983	Traffic count - 12,200 vehicles per day. Little Chalfont Community Day at Westwood Park.
1984	'Opening of M25 will not affect Little Chalfont' - BCC.
1985	Halifax House opened by Minister of Housing George Young in November. Amersham International Headquarters opened.
1988	Upper station car park extended. Daffodil planting scheme started.
1989	Village hall refurbished at cost of £50,000.
1991	Referendum on whether Little Chalfont should become a separate parish. Footpath from Long Walk to New Road approved.
1992	Over 2000 bluebell bulbs planted with help from the Brownies, supplementing earlier plantings. Houses built on former sports ground in Elizabeth Avenue.
1993	Railway station extensively refurbished. Newstead Hall at the Methodist Church destroyed by fire. Conifer trees in Westwood felled, leaving beeches to develop.

Index

Amersham Common: 6, 33, 34, 44, 45, 51, 59, 60, 66, 76, 82, 102, 121
Amersham Common Enclosure: 18
Amersham International: 78, 81, 105
Amersham Road: 69, 101
Amersham Town Council: 98
Amersham United Charities: 120
Amersham Way: 64, 69, 101
Ammunition Boxes: 97
Auntie's Property: 21

Bail Hall: 30, 35
Bails: 67
Baird, Thyra: 121
Barclays Bank: 67, 113
Bedford Avenue: 21, 50, 52, 76, 88, 101, 112, 121
Beechwood Avenue: 64, 101, 102
Beel Close: 104
Beel House: 6, 16, 17, 18, 19, 20, 28, 33, 46, 113, 114
Beel Lodge: 30, 32, 45, 59
Beel House Nurseries: 22, 45
Beer Shops: 45
Bell Lane: 33, 35, 44, 50, 62, 75, 101, 119, 122
Bell Lane Bonanza: 112
Bell Lane School: 112
Belle Vue School: 111, 112
Berkley Butchers: 67, 122
Bertram Mills Circus: 78, 87, 88, 105
Birkett Way: 104
Black Horse Bridge: 22, 121
Black Jack: 75
Blue Bells: 127
Blue Roof: 105
Bogarde, Dirk: 16
Bombers: 91 to 94
Bottle Cottage: 23
Boughtons: 59, 75, 82, 102
Bowler, Mr: 66, 119
Brickworks: 45
Brownies: 97, 99
Bryant, Burgess: 14
Bunkers Green: 66
Burtons Farm: 44, 120
Burtons Lane: 22, 35, 44, 45, 60, 67, 101, 104, 111, 121
Burtons Way: 22
Burtons Wood: 45
Burying Ground: 45
By-Pass: 102

Calves Crate: 21
Camp, Mlle: 68, 111
Carters Wood: 45
Cary's Map: 30
Catholic Church: 112
Catholic Players: 114
Cavendish: 6, 22, 28, 119
Central Way: 64
Chalfont Avenue: 113
Chalfont Road Station: 50, 51, 59, 60, 66
Chalfont Station Village: 62, 65, 68
Chalfont & Latimer Station: 52, 76
Chapel: 112
Chapel Field: 14, 45
Chapman: 76, 121
Chenies: 6, 34, 49, 101, 111
Chenies Avenue: 44, 64, 101, 102, 112
Chenies Estate: 64
Chenies Parade: 59, 102, 104
Chesham Lane: 33, 34
Chesham, Lord: 60, 75, 104, 119
Chessfield Park: 20, 69, 102
Chess Valley: 5, 35, 54, 101
Chess Valley Historical Society: 20
Chilcote House: 81
Chiltern Players: 99
Churches: 112, 113, 114
Church Grove: 34, 35, 44, 64, 69, 88, 91, 101
Church Grove Estate: 69
Clayton Walk: 104
Clifton Brothers: 67, 78
Coal Depot: 52
Cokes Farm: 6, 44, 45
Cokes Lane: 22, 44, 59, 67, 68, 101, 105, 112, 119, 122
Colemans Farm: 6, 14, 44, 88
Collins, Father: 16, 114
Coronation: 101
Cosy Café: 67
Croft, The: 92
Cross Rail: 49, 55
Cullens: 62
Cumberland Close: 104

Daffodils: 127
Dell Farm: 20, 21, 44, 119
Dell Wood: 44
Diamond Appeal: 113
Dr. Challoner: 16, 45, 112
District Council: 60, 97, 98, 105, 106, 127
Doggetts: 45
Dunfee: 97
Duke of Bedford: 6, 22, 49, 60, 69, 119

Elaine: 68
Electric Trains: 54, 55
Elvey, G.R.: 16
Elizabeth Avenue: 101, 105, 106, 121
Enclosures: 33
ENSA Parties: 89

Fatalities: 104, 119
Fields: 45
Finch Lane:
6, 16, 18, 23, 33, 35, 45, 59, 62, 66, 75, 113, 119
Fire Hydrants: 66
Fisk: 67
Forestry Commission: 6
Four & Twenty Ashes: 121
Freeborn, Howard: 62, 65, 66, 69
Free Church: 112

Galatea: 52
Garden Reach: 79, 104
Gas Masks: 87
Gates: 68, 78
Gilberts: 81
Glaze, Constance: 68, 111
Glis-Glis: 98
Golden Hind: 68, 88
Green Belt: 5, 6, 101
Grimsdell's Tomb: 13, 14, 30, 43, 45
Grover's Engines: 59, 75, 119
Grover's taxis: 121
Guides: 99

Haddon, Mr: 59, 62, 67, 123
Halifax, Keith: 105, 106
Halifax House: 78
Hancock: 62
Harewood Downs Golf Club: 122
Harrison, Rex: 16
Hatfield House: 28
Heather Border: 127
Hill Farm: 6, 44
Home Guards: 87, 89, 91, 92, 93, 97
Homestead: 111
Horse Drawn Taxis: 51
Hunting Boxes: 54

Irene: 68

Kendall, Kay: 16
Kenway Drive: 104
Kipling, Ken: 68, 78

Ladies Walk: 21
Latimer Avenue: 101, 112
Lerner, Alan: 16
Liberty Tomb: 14
Library: 122
Little Chalfont Café: 67
Little Chalfont Name: 65
Little Chalfont Sports Club: 105, 106
Little Chalfont Town Map: 6, 102
Little Reeves Farm: 16
Lloyds Bank: 67
Lodge Lane: 34, 50, 64, 121
Lofts: 67, 104
London Bus: 79
London Kiosks: 68
Long Walk: 104, 127
Loudhams Cottages: 45, 59
Loudhams Farm: 6, 22, 44, 59, 60, 104
Loudhams Lane: 35
Loudhams Road: 62, 88, 111
Lowndes, William: 13, 16, 18
Lucas, Benjamin: 21
Lyle Family: 18

Mair, Margaret: 21
Maplefield: 45
Marston, Colonel: 78, 97
Mason, Kender: 18, 28, 33, 34
Mayflower: 52
Meadows: 67
Methodist Church: 113
Metropolitan Railway:
44, 49 to 55, 59, 60, 63, 76
Metropolitan Railway Country Estates:
63, 64, 65
Metroland: 54, 64
Mile Post: 30
Milner Family: 18
Mission Church: 111, 112
Munn & Chapman: 67, 76, 97
My Fair Lady: 16

National Benzole Depot: 52
National Provincial Bank: 68
National School: 18, 111
Nelson, Lord: 18
Newstead Hall: 113
Nightingales Corner: 22, 34, 44, 66, 67, 88, 104
Nightingales Farm: 22, 121
Nightingales Lane: 81, 87, 105, 112

Oakington Avenue: 50, 69, 101, 121
Oakington Avenue School: 111
Oakwood Nursery: 68, 122
Oldfield Close: 101
Old House Farm: 6, 44, 59, 119
Opal Café: 68
Ordnance Survey: 65
Osbourne, Ozzy: 20
Oxford Stores: 62, 67, 82

Park Grove: 104
Penn, William: 16
Penningtons: 16
Peter Pans Parlour: 104, 122, 123
Phipps, Vicar: 50
Piece, The: 22

Pineapple Public House: 33, 45, 62, 102
Plummer (Green Grocer): 67
Polish Community: 14
Pollards Wood: 81, 87, 105
Pomeroy: 18
Population: 6, 69
Post Office: 62, 68, 101, 123
Praedial Tithes: 43
Priest's End: 45
Pucks Paigles: 121
Pucks Thatch: 112
Puggers: 45
Pullman Cars: 52
Puppet Theatre: 121

Quakers: 14, 16

Radio Chemicals: 81, 101
Railway Bridge: 55
Red Roofs: 112
Reeves Farm: 16
Reliance Shoes: 68, 122
Rendezvous: 62, 67, 122
Retreat, The: 121
Riffle Butts: 76
Road Widening: 67
Roman Roads: 27
Rook Pie: 123
Rocque's Map: 33, 35
Round House, The: 112
Royal Acts: 27, 28, 32, 43, 49
Rural District Council: 20, 60, 106
Russell, Thomas: 22
Russell Close: 101

St. Aidan's: 16, 113
St. George's: 111, 112
St. Nicholas Close: 68, 104, 111
St. Nicholas School: 68, 111
Salisbury, Lord: 28
Schools: 68, 111, 112
School Treat: 18
Sheep Houses: 20, 21, 45, 59, 69, 101, 119
ShenstoneHouse: 105
Shooting: 54
Snell's Charity: 21, 119
Snell's Farm: 6, 21, 44, 45
Snell's Lane: 33, 34, 45, 59
Snell's Wood: 44, 59, 127
Snell's Wood Court: 105
Sperlins Lane: 21
Springett, Gulielma: 16
Station Approach: 50, 68
Station Garages: 81, 88
Statter's Switchgear: 78, 79, 88, 89, 105, 122
Statter's Folies: 89
Stony Lane: 21, 27, 34, 102, 121
Street Lighting: 66
Stubwick Hedgerow: 44
Swannell & Sly: 68
Sugar Loaves: 67, 97, 113

Telephone Exchange: 68, 82, 83
Telephone Operators: 82
Ten Turrets: 79
Thames Bookshop: 122
Thatched Roofs: 62, 66
Thomas, Mrs Nancy: 22, 69, 91
Thomlinson, Father: 113
Thorium Ltd: 81
Tithe Map: 21, 23, 35, 43, 45, 104, 119
Tithe Commutation Act: 43
Tolls: 28, 30
Toll House: 5, 32
Tombs: 13, 14, 43, 45
Traffic Count: 66
Turnpike Road: 5, 21, 27 to 35, 50
Turnpike Trusts: 27, 34

Uxbridge Electricity Company: 66

Village Halls: 97 to 99
Village Way: 5, 50, 60, 65, 66, 67, 101, 111, 112

Washing: 69
Weatherill's: 67
West Indies: 46
Westminster Magazine: 61
Westwood Drive: 101
Westwood Park: 102, 106
Wheeler, Ivy: 66, 120
Wheelers: 63
White Cottage, The: 112
White Lion Inn: 20, 22, 27, 30, 32, 46, 59, 67, 81, 119, 121
White Lion Road: 62, 67, 79, 101, 104, 112, 113
Wilder, John: 30
Williams, Bryn: 20
William's Clothing: 88
Willmott's Farm: 6
Women's Institutes: 97, 98, 122
Woodside House: 17

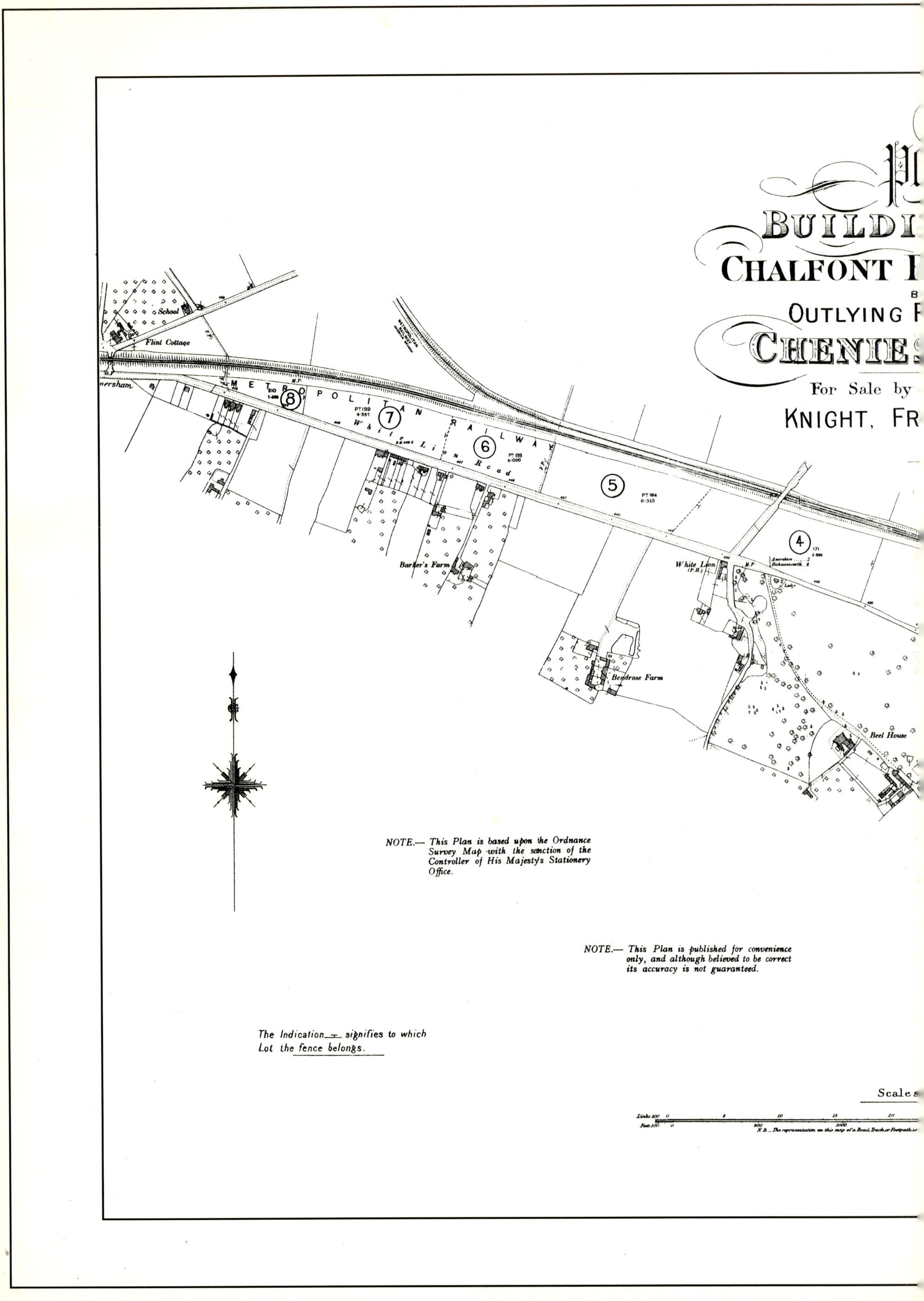
BUILDI
CHALFONT F
OUTLYING F
CHENIES
For Sale by
KNIGHT, FR
School
Flint Cottage
METROPOLITAN RAILWAY
White Lion Road
Barker's Farm
Bendrose Farm
White Lion (P.H.)
Beel House
NOTE.— This Plan is based upon the Ordnance Survey Map with the sanction of the Controller of His Majesty's Stationery Office.
NOTE.— This Plan is published for convenience only, and although believed to be correct its accuracy is not guaranteed.
The Indication signifies to which Lot the fence belongs.
Scale